179611

£17.99

UNIVERSITY COLLEGE BIRMINGHAM
COLLEGE LIBRARY, SUMMER ROW
BIRMINGHAM. B3 1JB
Tel: (0121) 243 0055

DATE OF RETURN

Please remember to return on time or pay the fine

D1440037

SHORT GUIDES TO RISK SERIES

Risk is a far more complex and demanding issue than it was ten years ago. Risk managers may have expertise in the general aspects of risk management and in the specifics that relate directly to their business, but they are much less likely to understand other more specialist risks. Equally, Company Directors may find themselves falling down in their duty to manage risk because they don't have enough knowledge to be able to talk to their risk team in a sensible way.

The short guides to risk are not going to make either of these groups experts in the subject but will give them plenty to get started and in a format and an extent (circa 100 pages) that is readily digested.

Titles in the series will include:

- Climate Risk
- Compliance Risk
- Employee Risk
- Environmental Risk
- Fraud Risk
- Information Risk
- Intellectual Property Risk
- Kidnap and Ransom Risk
- Operational Risk
- Purchasing Risk
- Reputation Risk
- Strategic Risk
- Supply Chain Risk
- Tax Risk
- Terrorism Risk

For further information, visit www.gowerpublishing.com/shortguidestorisk

A Short Guide to Reputation Risk

Garry Honey

GOWER

Published by
Gower Publishing Limited
Wey Court East
Union Road
Farnham
Surrey GU9 7PT
England

Gower Publishing Company
Suite 420
101 Cherry Street
Burlington, VT 05401-4405
USA

www.gowerpublishing.com

British Library Cataloguing in Publication Data
Honey, Garry
   A short guide to reputation risk. -- (Short guide to
   business risk)
   1. Corporate image--Management. 2. Risk management.
   I. Title II. Series
   659.2-dc22

   ISBN: 978-0-566-08995-4

Library of Congress Cataloging-in-Publication Data
Honey, Garry.
   A short guide to reputation risk / by Garry Honey.
     p. cm. -- (Short guide to business risk)
   Includes bibliographical references and index.
   ISBN 978-0-566-08995-4 (pbk) -- ISBN 978-0-566-08996-1 1. Risk assessment.
   2. Risk management. 3. Corporate image. 4. Intangible property--Valuation.
   I. Title.
   HD61.H556 2009
   659.2--dc22

                  2009010438

Mixed Sources
Product group from well-managed
forests and other controlled sources
www.fsc.org Cert no. SA-COC-1565
© 1996 Forest Stewardship Council

Printed and bound in Great Britain by
MPG Books Group, UK

Contents

List of Figures

1 The Nature and Value of Reputation

Talk of reputation is most commonly associated with damage. A reputation attaches itself to a person, place or organisation and can be damaged accidentally. Damage of course destroys value whether this is financial or more intangible: esteem or prestige. It is this destruction of value that makes news; an increase makes for a dull story.

Definitions of reputation are not hard to find. Here is one from *Invisible Advantage* by Jonathan Low and Pam Cohen Kalafut:

> *In a sense a company's reputation is the ultimate intangible. It's literally nothing more than how the organisation is perceived by a variety of people. It is slippery, volatile, easily compromised, impossible to control, amorphous.*

I like this definition because it admits reputation is hard to pin down in monetary terms, despite the fact that damage ultimately carries a cost. It makes reputation risk a particular challenge to internal auditors and risk managers.

Reputation is a term that is over-used by journalists, and often incorrectly used within organisations themselves. Reputation is not synonymous with brand, goodwill or even image. A brand is a consumer proposition created and managed by its owner in order to generate revenue. A reputation is a perception held by others about you, in anticipation of future behaviour. The two could not be more different in terms of ownership, control or purpose.

Goodwill is an accountancy term for the intangible value of customer loyalty. Image is a one-dimensional mental picture or snapshot without the future or historic element present in reputation.

In order to appreciate fully the nature of reputation I use six simple aspects. This is based on the acronym REPUTE and it may help you get a handle on the slippery, volatile and amorphous side of its nature.

Relational construct – You have a reputation with somebody for something. In a domestic context your wife will expect you to behave as a husband, your daughter will expect you to behave as a father, and so on. In a commercial world your organisation has stakeholders – those groups of people who are affected in some way by your actions. Each group has a unique relationship with your business, a unique perspective and a distinct expectation.

Most businesses consider their reputation with shareholders or investors to be the most critical, after all investor confidence is reflected through market capitalization and share price. Nevertheless reputation with customers, suppliers or employees is equally important, as without any one of these the business would cease to exist. Stakeholder groups that create value are called primary, as distinct from those that merely influence value (secondary).

It is possible to have more than one reputation. Consider a major grocery chain with attractive retail prices for customers achieved through squeezing supplier margins; a good reputation with customers for value can result in a poor reputation with suppliers. Perception depends on where you stand. City investors may rate your business for its ability to deliver dividends, however employees might feel that this is achieved at the expense of salaries that are below market average.

Is reputation with one group more important than another? Should you take notice of all stakeholder concerns? Is there a hierarchy? Should you prioritise? These are strategic questions the board should be asking. Stakeholder relationship management is taking over from customer relationship management as a business focus. One leading CEO defined a stakeholder as: 'anyone who can bugger up your business'.

Exception attributed – Reputation is attributed for some action or behavioural characteristic that sets you apart from competitors or peers, it is both a perception of character and differentiator. Among investors it may be for delivering forecast dividends as promised; among customers it might be for delivering value-for-money consistently; among employees it might be for providing a generous pension plan. Reputation is for a specific activity that others won't or can't match. In one sense this is reputation as notoriety.

Attributing reputation by exception presumes that the stakeholder group has some knowledge of competitors and peers in order to make the comparison. Take for example the previous case of a corporation with a reputation for delivering forecast dividends: if every operator in the sector delivered forecast dividends then this would not suffice as a differentiator, investors would choose a different characteristic. Stakeholders use reputation as a differentiating tool not unlike a brand name.

Reputation by exception must also be seen against the background of stereotypes. For example, banks are seen as risk averse, cautious and prudent organisations, a safe haven for your money. A reckless bank should be conspicuous by its behaviour as exceptional (although we live in exceptional times when quite a few were shown to have been bigger risk takers than expected). Reputation management is about managing expectation and avoiding surprises which draw attention to performance above or below expectation.

Consider the fact that we tend to trust bishops and headmasters more than estate agents or car salesmen. We are therefore more disgusted when those in whom we place greater than average trust betray us. Reputation is a relative concept and reflects the environment in which we operate as much as our own actions.

Perception comparison – Reputation is based on a perception, it doesn't have to rely on truth or reality but on a combination of the experience, knowledge and belief of stakeholders. An organisation has the capacity to improve a stakeholder experience and some ability to improve stakeholder knowledge but relatively little power to influence belief. If a stakeholder group believes your organisation is incompetent or fraudulent, there is very little you can do to dissuade it.

4

We have seen that reputation is attributed by exception, so that a norm or benchmark exists against which this behaviour is deemed exceptional. I have seen employee surveys that show employees think they are paid below the sector average, despite the evidence to the contrary. If your organisation pays its employees in line with industry averages, this will matter little if the employees believe their pay is lower. The net result will be a poor reputation among employees.

Perception changes over time and with changes to the business environment. For example, a few years ago a social responsibility policy was a differentiator in itself, however today every major corporation publishes one. This (in itself) is no longer a guarantee of a good reputation but merely an expected business output like an annual report. Reputation does not exist in a vacuum; it is vulnerable to the evolution of stakeholder expectation. Managing this expectation requires engagement with stakeholders to improve perceptions.

Unintended consequences – Nobody sets out to damage their reputation or reduce their own value. Granted some third parties might have an interest in driving down the value of a corporation from which they intend to profit, but no organisation sets out to damage its own good reputation on purpose. Damage is almost invariably the result of a sequence of actions the outcome of which is inadvertently detrimental.

Fear of reputation damage focuses on good turning to bad, not bad turning good. Quality, on the other hand, manifests itself in many ways not obviously good and bad. For example, a reputation for supporting good causes may make you appear philanthropic. If next year all your peers contributed significantly more to charities then your contribution might

5

look miserly. Activity by others can influence the quality of your reputation: you may not do anything and your reputation quality could be reduced by exception and perception.

It follows that something of which you can justifiably be proud today becomes something of which you could suddenly be ashamed tomorrow. This volatility of reputation is something that corporations ignore at their peril. Reputation management requires constant vigilance. A good reputation is not easily won and commonly hard earned. A bad one of course can attach itself quickly and prove very sticky.

Building a good reputation is not something that many organisations do consciously, as a good reputation is a by-product of good management. Organisations that acquire a good reputation do so because they are managing the issues which are business critical not necessarily reputation critical. Attempting to manage reputation in itself is inadvisable and rarely successful, stakeholders soon become aware that reputation is more important than the business itself and this destroys trust. Effective reputation management is discreet and subtle.

Unintended consequences abound: who would have thought that the raising of the inter-bank lending rate in August 2007 would have created waves throughout the global economy? Hindsight is a wonderful perspective but before the run on Northern Rock, funds could be raised in the wholesale market and nobody predicted this would cease overnight.

The law of unintended consequences states that for every action there will always be some consequences that were unintended. We simply need to become more effective at predicting all the implications of our actions if we are to protect reputation successfully.

Track record – A reputation is built over time based on an activity trend. Predicting behaviour through extrapolating from this trend is what sets out the quality of a reputation. Leopards don't change their spots and many organisations have a culture that can't change overnight, in most cases behaviour will be predictable.

Communication is important with stakeholders and an external relations function is valuable, however it is not what we say but what we do that determines reputation. Stakeholders judge an organisation on its behaviour not its claims. They are also more likely to believe media comment – which they see as independent – rather than stories put out by the company itself.

It follows that reputation management should not be the responsibility of corporate communications. Reputation is about behaviour and corporate culture. Stakeholders can be alienated by 'spin' and news management. Reputation depends on people and the HR department is a natural home for reputation management, more so than the PR department.

Where a disconnect exists between how an organisation behaves and what it communicates to the outside world, then there is ample scope for reputation damage. There is a common belief that reputation can be repaired after an event through crisis management and damage limitation activity, however this is always expensive. Stakeholders know that lasting change in corporate behaviour will not happen overnight.

Emotional appeal – A good reputation is a valuable endorsement of trust. Damage to reputation occurs when our trust is shown to have been misplaced and disillusionment sets in. We expect our money safe in a bank, and children safe with a teacher. So when we talk of damaged reputation we actually mean that we made a mistake and placed trust in someone that ultimately wasn't justified. Were we let down by a poor performance or did we expect too much in the first place?

When our value judgement, which is based on experience, fails us our confidence is eroded. This is why errant teachers and bankers make headlines. It is because our expectations of them are comparatively higher than of others, in whom we don't place as much trust. The better the reputation the more vulnerable it is and the more susceptible to damage. The principle of 'The higher you are the further you fall' applies.

Reputation dictates how people behave and in whom they place trust. Once this trust is lost it is almost impossible to regain. Damage to reputation correlates positively with trust recovery. Damage is greatest where trust is difficult to regain as in cases of fraud, conversely it is slightest where trust recovery can be achieved easily, for example, after a minor incident.

Trust in any relationship requires predictable behaviour and 'no surprises'. There is a fairly close correlation between ethical behaviour and a good reputation. This is because trust requires both a mutual understanding of right and wrong, linked to a determination to do the right thing irrespective of cost.

THE VALUE OF REPUTATION

The value of reputation is frequently under-estimated because it is rarely measured. In many global corporations it is the silent asset that only shows up in the gap between book value and market capitalization. A significant part of the Intellectual Capital of a firm, reputation has enormous value in attracting new customers, employees and investors. Often a hidden boost to marketing and advertising activity of an organisation, nobody knows the true value of reputation in securing future revenue or maintaining market share.

At the time of writing, national governments across the world are stepping in to prop up banks in order to restore confidence in the banking industry, something that would have been unthinkable a year ago. This shows how much we rely on trust. We place our savings in a bank and trust that they will be there next week. Without trust there is no commerce, the high inter-bank lending rate reflects the distrust that still persists among banks.

Outside of the banking industry, the public sector has worries of its own. Government departments have been in the news for losing sensitive data entrusted to them and subsequently lost in transit between offices or contractor sites. What does this say about the trust placed in government by the general public? A government keen to introduce strict security measures and ID cards does not set a confidence boosting example. Does it enjoy a good reputation for security of our personal data?

In the professions where the partnership structure operates, reputation depends on client service and value for money. Reputation rests largely on the shoulders of partners, their teams' expertise, and the combined ability to deliver both client satisfaction and fee income. Reputation of a professional firm relies on integrity as much as competence. How clients expect partners to behave is fundamental to quality of reputation. Professionalism underpins a good reputation, but can professionalism be defined any more than reputation?

There is no doubt that reputation has a value but it manages to avoid tangible measurement. However, there are two ways to measure reputation value. One is the monetary valuation applied to an intangible asset for either insurance or risk purposes. This approach which uses Market Capitalisation or Return on Assets modelling often attracts the attention of the CEO or Finance Director. It is a method that requires so many assumptions and caveats that the final figure is rarely meaningful. The alternative approach involves the relative valuation of reputation as intellectual capital for internal performance using score cards or similar indices. This can be an interesting exercise but may lead to a complex list of up to 100 different variables with subjective weighting.

To conclude, the value of reputation may be best expressed in terms of magnetism. A good reputation attracts and a bad reputation repels. A good reputation is slowly earned amongst stakeholders, a bad one is quickly assigned by the same stakeholders. An organisation or business has little control over its reputation, however it should understand that not all stakeholder groups share the same perspective. This implies that reputation is multifaceted and it offers a clue to reputation management – exploit the ones you have.

SUMMARY

Reputation is something you are given by others, you do not choose it, others assign it to you so its quality is a reflection of how they see you. You can of course influence how others see you by your behaviour, but a reputation is earned as a consequence of actions. It is a secondary feature that can become part of your identity among stakeholders.

The quality of reputation is determined by your behaviour, good or bad, within the context of your market or local environment. This quality is comparative and depends as much on the reputation of rivals as it does on your own. To achieve a good reputation it is first necessary to understand what a bad one would look like in your market. Opposites play an important role in expressing reputation quality.

② The Causes and Impact of Reputation Risk

It follows that if a reputation has value, then anything that can reduce this value represents a risk. This is the basis on which reputation risk is generally perceived – something that can cause damage. Unfortunately this is indicative of how many people perceive risk as something to be avoided or controlled, certainly not something to encourage or invite. Entrepreneurs and investors may have a very different view. They seek out risk in order to make gains and create wealth.

Risk to reputation is generally understood to mean the uncertainty surrounding circumstances in which a good reputation may become 'tarnished' tainted or reduced in some way. Technically of course there is a converse risk of a bad reputation being improved which implies risk is an opportunity not a threat. This is rarely seen or recognised as reputation risk, being more likely a 'stroke of luck'. So reputation risk is commonly seen as a risk of value reduction not value increment.

Is there a definition of reputation risk? Yes, reputation risk involves an organisation acting, behaving or performing in a way that falls short of stakeholder expectations. Risk sits in the gap between stakeholder expectation and company performance. Managing the risk is all about closing, or trying to minimise, this gap. This simple explanation is complicated by the fact that different stakeholder groups have different expectations depending on their perspective and concerns.

Stakeholder expectations are not a static commodity; they are fickle and subject to other influences including media exposure, market knowledge, and competitor claims. The only certainty is that expectations normally go up not down, it is rare for stakeholders to expect less of you year on year. This implies the need to anticipate where and how stakeholder expectations will shift and deliver against them: under-delivery is clearly a risk but over-delivery is an extravagant waste. Efficient management is about alignment of values to reduce risk (see Figure 2.1).

Alignment risk

Current Performance	Nature of risk	Action needed	
Exceeding expectation	Risk as opportunity	Align to *exploit*	Exploit
Slightly above expectation	Risk as opportunity	Align to *exploit*	
Meeting expectations	No risk	In alignment	
Slightly below expectations	Risk as threat	Align to *improve*	Improve
Falling below expectation	Risk as threat	Align to *improve*	

Figure 2.1   Aligning reputation risk and performance

Risk to reputation is caused by a misalignment of values; the organisation failing in some way to meet stakeholder expectations head on, delivering either significantly above or below expectation. As reputation is a relational concept this failure can manifest itself in a number of different ways from mild disappointment to extreme outrage. The risk is value based (just as relationships are) not cost based and it cannot be expressed in this way.

Stakeholders have expectations and damage to our relationship with them depends on how much our behaviour diverges from their expectations. Where trust is completely *lost* and cannot be regained outrage is a likely response; for example, an act of major fraud, particularly in an institution where trust is implicit such as a charity. Conversely trust may be *questioned* prompting stakeholder disappointment, a situation from which it is possible to recover given time, money and some forgiveness. It is rarely damaging in the long term.

I find it useful to image a scale of stakeholder response, using ratings from 1–5, not unlike the hurricane severity scale used in the US. This enables you to express damage in relation to trust destroyed as a result of performance under-delivery (see Figure 2.2).

The extent of any damage depends both on how much trust is lost and also on the time, effort, patience and cost required to regain this trust. Damage severity can be extreme or slight depending on three things: a) quality of reputation prior to the incident; b) the cause of the incident and c) the handling of the incident to prevent it becoming a crisis (Figure 2.3).

If your reputation enjoys a reservoir of goodwill prior to an incident, if the incident was clearly not your fault and could

5 levels of stakeholder response

Level	Stakeholder reaction	Trust damage	Characteristics
5	Outrage	**Trust completely lost** – not recoverable	Fraud, embezzlement, illegal or criminal activity
4	Disgust	**Trust severely damaged** – never fully recoverable	Incompetence, poor management decision making
3	Concern	**Trust diminished** – recoverable at considerable cost	Accident or safety issue e.g. product recall
2	Surprise	**Trust dented** – recoverable with time and good PR	Poor judgement or lack of control e.g. supply chain problems
1	Disappointment	**Trust questioned** – but recoverable speedily	Inconsistent behaviour e.g. gap between policy and reality

Figure 2.2   The relative scale of reputation damage

3 factors influencing damage

3 key factors	aspects	qualification
1. Existing goodwill Prior state of trust	– Quantity – Quality – Dependent conditions	Quality before an event – accumulated goodwill or 'forgiveness factor'
2. Nature of threat Impact event or crisis	– Cause – Preventability – Containability	Whose fault? Blame and culpability as influencers
3. Response to threat Reaction and crisis handling	– Efficiency – Comprehensiveness – Sensitivity	Immediate and unquestioning response – e.g. product recall

Figure 2.3   Relative severity of reputation damage

not reasonably have been predicted or prevented, or if your response is immediate, comprehensive and compassionate then very little damage should result.

A potentially damaging incident may be contained and defused through luck and quick action, but equally a minor incident can escalate if it is poorly handled. Those who believe that local problems stay local under-estimate the capacity of bad news to travel fast – only good news stays local.

The impact of reputation risk therefore depends on the cost of recovering trust, and the consequent risk impact grid is similar to the stakeholder response scale. The key difference is that in risk impact terms trust *recovery*, as opposed to trust *damage*, is the determining factor. Below is an example of a risk impact grid designed to enable a global corporation to add reputation to the risk register (Figure 2.4).

Reputation risk is thus 'a risk to value in a relationship of trust, where the cost of the risk is the cost of recovering lost trust'. How do you protect this trust? The answer is expectation management. Where expectations are aligned with performance there can be no risk and therefore no surprises – which is the mantra of all truly transparent organisations. In any relationship we have expectations which subsequently may or may not prove to be correct. Where they prove correct we have no surprises, but where they prove incorrect we have surprise. Everything depends on our expectation at the outset (Figure 2.5).

Can you put a price on lost trust or the damage it causes? Most analysts rely on the drop in share price or market capitalisation as a tangible indication of reputation damage. This is not the whole picture but is understandably newsworthy as it

Risk register

Trust recovery is key to reputation risk classification

Risk impact	Reputation damage profile
Very low	Trust recoverable with little effort or cost – a minor blip on the radar.
	Risk containable locally – no need to involve senior management, keep informed.
Low	Trust recoverable at modest cost with resource allocation within budgets.
	Risk containable at sector level – senior management to be kept informed.
Medium	Trust recovery demands cost authorisation above and beyond existing budgets.
	Risk containable at group sector level – senior management involved.
High	Trust recoverable at considerable cost and management attention.
	Risk demands immediate attention – dedicated budget and staff.
Very High	Trust severely damaged and full recovery questionable and costly.
	Risk demands attention of group board and priority action.

Figure 2.4   The risk impact grid

Reputation dynamics

	Negative Experience	Positive Experience
High Expectation	*Destruction* Surprise and disappointment Reputation worsened	*Reinforcement* High expectation rewarded Good reputation sustained
Low Expectation	*Reinforcement* Low expectations endorsed Bad reputation sustained	*Construction* Surprise and inspiration Reputation enhanced

Threats

opportunities

Figure 2.5   Expectation and risk

translates into millions of pounds. Share price represents reputation with one group, at one moment in time and it excludes the reputation damage which will show as a future cost: declines in future customer revenue, employee morale and supplier confidence which all have a cost that will impact in subsequent financial reporting.

Short term damage can be seen financially in the cost to recover confidence either of investors, customers or other key stakeholders. Cost of lost sales, product recall or operational on-costs can all be allocated to reputation damage cost, but these are essentially short term in comparison to the longer term cost of damaged trust. Nobody knows how many future sales are lost when customers switch to more reliable brands or service providers.

Talk of reputation damage makes for emotive headlines but fails to cut much ice with risk or finance people who want to know the cost of a damaging event. Herein lies the problem, reputation damage is not caused by an event, it is caused by a misalignment of expectation and delivery. If reputation damage were caused by a single event then it could be covered by insurance. As reputation cannot be priced, it follows that damage to it cannot be priced. Reputation damage is an emotional expression of value reduction which impacts over time.

There are at least six different possible sources of reputation damage. To understand these it is first necessary to identify four different types of risk handling strategies, to three of which reputation risk is relevant.

FOUR RISK HANDLING STRATEGIES

TRANSFER

Some risk can be transferred through insurance or other vehicles such as securitisation. The financial crisis which became the 'Credit Crunch' was caused by excessive risk transfer. Consumer debt in the form of mortgages with a relatively high risk of default was repackaged as low risk and sold as securitisation on wholesale financial markets worldwide. The risk was passed around until none of the banks knew exactly how much potential default each was carrying. The interbank lending rate crept up to reflect this mutual distrust and the most highly leveraged banks suffered.

Some risk can be transferred but only if the party taking it on is fully cognisant of the extent of the financial liability and probability of exposure. Mortgage debt repackaged as triple A security was nowhere near as safe a risk as ratings agencies indicated. Creative product development took caution out of risk leading to reckless investment by leading banks.

Reputation however cannot be insured as the owner represents a 'moral hazard' who can significantly influence both the probability of a claim and the extent of any loss. Reputation risk is essentially behavioural and cannot be passed to a third party. Insurers have not yet found a satisfactory policy formula to cover reputation risk.

AVOID

Much of what passes for enterprise risk management (ERM) is in reality a system for identifying and avoiding risk which can have a negative financial impact. Avoiding risk is how most risk managers see their roles in business. Preventing cost damage liability through a system of checks and balances designed to avoid risk. Cynics have said that risk management as a discipline is fast becoming one of managing the avoidance of risk not actually one of managing risk itself.

Avoiding risk comes naturally in the workplace where Health and Safety regulations set in place a code for common sense personal safety. As a behavioural risk, reputation risk can and should be avoided but the risk can sometimes seem too obvious to notice. A workplace environment that is driven by sales or profit growth can expose itself to ethical and even legal problems.

We may think we can spot the next Enron or Barings but in reality the legal boundaries are subject to interpretation, for example, the difference between tax avoidance and evasion. In the same way as banks encouraged complex investment vehicles to create wealth, so too the accountancy firms encourage clients to minimise tax liability to retain wealth.

MANAGE

Some risk has to be managed because it cannot be outsourced or transferred to a third party, it is inherent within the operation of the organisation. Think of employee relations, human capital and people risk. These have two sub-categories, executive and operations, both of which are normally fully accounted for under the remit of internal audit or risk management teams within any organisation. Failure at either level can usually be traced to failure of quality process or internal vigilance.

Executive risk is expressed as the quality of decision making by the board or management team. Any shortfall in performance can usually be dealt with by shareholders or institutional investors through changing Chair or CEO with the remit to shake up the team.

Operational risk is more common in manufacturing and distribution channels where a fault in the production process leads to a product recall. The risk to reputation occurs when a recall indicates that product quality is no longer as consistent as the brand name implies.

Damaging risk to reputation is rare within the category of managerial risk. This is because the systems are normally already in place and the fault can easily be traced and remedied. Most serious reputational damage happens in two other categories, cultural (avoidable) and external (mitigable).

MITIGATE

Some risks lie outside the organisation's direct control yet the nature of business and its dependence on suppliers, agents, contractors and other third parties means that the organisation has no choice in accepting the risks. For these risks the strategy must be reduction or mitigation as the organisation has no direct control over them. External risks can come from a business relationship or a natural hazard in the environment.

Natural hazards such as fire and flood usually cause less reputation damage than actual physical damage. Customers and suppliers are usually sympathetic to a business hit by fire or flood (unless of course the cause is believed to be negligence). The financial damage of a flood or fire can be covered by insurance but the reputation damage from closure is more difficult to cover.

The risk to reputation from association with a supplier or partner whose actions can damage your organisation is dramatically but correctly termed 'contamination risk'. Think here of British Airways and their contract caterers Gate Gourmet a few years ago, the actions of a supplier damaged the reputation of the airline. Business partners must be chosen to align with the sponsor's values or else provide grounds for contamination damage.

Imagine you are an un-named law firm whose whole reputation rests on the motorcycle courier contractor you have selected to deliver critical documents to clients, courts and counsel. If the contractor doesn't share your values of punctuality, fastidiousness, courtesy or whatever, there is a chance you will suffer the consequences of this value conflict. One of the biggest contamination risks today lies in outsourcing customer services to call centres. Irrespective of whether the call centre is in Glasgow or Bombay, customer service should be a core function of a sustainable business and not peripheral.

SIX CAUSES OF REPUTATION RISK

Having looked at the four types of risk handling strategy and recognised that only three apply to reputation risk, it is worth expressing these three (avoid, manage, mitigate) from the perspective of the sources of risk to give us six separate causes of reputation risk (see Figure 2.6)

6 causes of reputation damage

Cultural		Managerial		External	
Risks to avoid		Risks to manage		Risks to mitigate	
Legal	Ethical	Executive	Operations	Associations	Environment
Imposed by external regulator	Self imposed codes of conduct	Senior management decision making	Middle management functional activity	Third party actions contamination risk	Commercial or physical impact

Behavioural risk
Examine process
Beyond governance
Value misalignment

Partnering risk
Risk by association
People & organisations
Value conflict

Figure 2.6   Sources of risk and management strategies

1. Cultural – Legal

2. Cultural – Ethical

3. Managerial – Executive

4. Managerial – Operations

5. External – Associations

6. External – Environment

The two most interesting areas for reputation risk are highlighted: ethical and associations.

ETHICAL

Cultural/ethical risks are intra-company and involve different departments or business units that espouse contradictory values and risk the reputation of the organisation as a whole. Here there is often a behavioural *risk* in the procedures and supervision that can damage an organisation. The risk lies in value misalignment with the company core values.

A Canadian drug firm with an ethical policy introduced new sales targets to its telesales team but soon found that customers were concerned about the pressure they were under and the claims being made for the drug. An investigation found that the pressure to achieve targets had led the sales force to act beyond the ethical boundaries of the company. A value misalignment had occurred between the company values and those of its own workers.

The risk was identified through examining the process, not simply in terms of basic governance and looking at value misalignment within the organisation. The risk was under the noses of management but apparently invisible to them.

ASSOCIATION

External/association risks are inter-company and involve partner organisations with whom we operate jointly and who represent a contamination risk where their behaviour may impact our reputation. The risk here is in the case of the values of the people and organisations with whom we work showing little or no alignment with our own. In some cases there may be a value conflict. This misalignment needs to be identified and recognised as a reputation risk.

As an example, imagine an outsourced call centre. The values of its management are rarely the same as its sponsoring client. Knowledge of products and services is never as good as the parent company. My water supplier's call centre was based in India and offered a very prompt online enquiry service, the only problem was the call centre employees didn't know how my meter worked or how the company billed me.

The values of third parties can never be identical to those of a sponsor. The risk lies in the scale of the gap and the quality of the strategy for mitigating it. Audits of contamination risk show just how this risk can balloon into serious reputation damage. Inevitably the figures that support an outsourcing decision never allow for intangible risk and rarely show how much risk exists in a small cost saving.

SUMMARY

Reputation risk sits in the gap between performance and expectation. Managing the risk lies in management of expectation among stakeholders as much as it does in performance. The key to expectation management is alignment. Where expectation is too high or too low then reputation is likely to suffer damage. Stakeholder response will depend on the size of misalignment: if great it could be outrage, if little it could be disappointment. This is the impact of reputation risk.

The cause of reputation risk is most commonly either internal misalignment of values or external value conflict. The former occurs where the operating culture of an organisation is at variance with its own values or behaviour codes; the latter occurs where an external third party, acting on behalf of the organisation, fails to deliver the same value as expected and thus contaminates reputation through this conflict of values.

3 Identifying Stakeholders and Risk Drivers

Measuring reputation risk is not as easy as it sounds and is certainly not the same as measuring reputation itself which has a different purpose. Anyone expressing an interest in measuring reputation should be questioned about the ultimate value of this information. What is the purpose of measuring reputation? There are two distinctly different routes to take: financial and non-financial and the choice of technique is dependent on the objectives of the exercise.

Putting a monetary measurement on reputation implies a valuation. There are those who believe that if a brand can be valued so too can a reputation. Sadly it is not so simple. As an intangible asset it would be extremely helpful to identify a monetary value for reputation. Valuation methodologies such as Market Capitalisation or Return on Asset analyses do offer a monetary measurement for reputation, the only problem is that there are so many assumptions in the formula that a final figure is rarely meaningful. There is no single accepted methodology.

A non-financial measure of reputation is likely to be more useful if your aim is to explore the Intellectual Capital (IC) value of reputation within the organisation. Using a score card method, anything from 10 to 100 variables can be measured comparatively to demonstrate where social or non-financial value lies within it. Scandinavian academics such as Edvinsson and Sveiby pioneered an approach to Intellectual Capital and their work can be found on Knowledge Management (KM) website such as Gurteen (www.gurteen.com). Measuring reputation as a non-financial value in an IC matrix can help HR and Organisation Behaviour specialists understand the complex social nature of an organisation. Reputation is measured as a relative value but not an absolute one.

Reputation *risk,* on the other hand, is relatively easy to measure. It sits in the gap between stakeholder expectation and corporate performance. Where there is scope for surprise or disappointment there also lies reputation risk. Where stakeholder expectation is higher than performance or behaviour this causes disappointment, which may require performance improvement to close the gap. Conversely where the expectation is lower than performance there is also risk, however this takes the form of a pleasant surprise and is normally far less damaging. In this case the risk is an opportunity as opposed to a threat. The gap harbours the risk but the level of stakeholder expectation determines whether this risk is a threat or an opportunity. Most people consider risk as a threat when they talk of reputation risk.

Measuring reputation risk is thus an exercise in gap analysis, the challenge is to find a currency for indexing stakeholder expectation, which has both meaning in itself and as a comparator, with corporate performance. Performance is often expressed financially but it is anticipated behaviour we should measure and this is not always financial. Measuring expectation among any stakeholder group requires an understanding of stakeholder attitudes and the relationship each group has with your organisation. Thus, it is necessary to survey stakeholder expectation in terms of *perception* and not in terms of customer or employee *satisfaction*, as is so often the case.

STAKEHOLDERS

At this point it is perhaps appropriate to define the term 'stakeholder'. The word is not yet in common usage across all departments in many organisations, although Investor Relations and Corporate Communications people generally have a good understanding. A stakeholder is *'anyone who can affect or be affected by your organisation'* this covers a large number of types of connections from customers and employees to local councils and business neighbours. Stakeholders are 'issue determined' and are self defining for any specific issue. For example, if your company is building a new factory then a stakeholder for its construction will be the local authority planning department. This department is unlikely to be a stakeholder for any other aspect of the business, and will probably only be a stakeholder for the duration of the construction.

The number of stakeholders an organisation has can vary significantly depending on its size and scope. In the public sector, organisations such as the NHS have a myriad of stakeholders but some private companies can manage with as few as ten. The most important distinction is between primary and secondary. Primary stakeholders are essential to the business, without them it would cease to be a viable business. Typically there are at least four groups of primary stakeholders: investors, employees, customers and suppliers. Take away one of these and the business will not survive for long.

Secondary stakeholders play an important role and can influence the value of an organisation. Trade unions, the media, regulators and local or national government fall into the category of secondary stakeholders. Without any one of these the business might not be the same but it could survive. The challenge for most commercial enterprises is to identify correctly the number of different stakeholder groups. A stakeholder group is of course a collection of stakeholders sharing the same defining perspective or issue.

One final point on stakeholder groups is worth noting. A group is not a homogeneous or exclusive unit, for example, it is possible to be both an investor and a customer. Furthermore in some industries, such as defence, it is possible to find one stakeholder, the government, playing three distinct stakeholder roles: policy maker, regulator and customer. Be aware that stakeholder group labels can be misleading and that the people can be in more than one group at a time.

STAKEHOLDER MAPPING

For most organisations there is no simple, single hierarchy of stakeholders but more often a matrix of stakeholders reflecting different degrees of influence over and interest in the organisation (see Figure 3.1). Mapping stakeholders against these two determinants helps to prioritise communications and prevent accidental reputation damage. Communication strategies that aim to avoid reputation risk recognise that interest in the organisation is within the control of the communications team. However the power and influence of a stakeholder audience lies outside their control. A typical communication strategy will therefore aim to move stakeholders from the left to right-hand side boxes, working on increasing the interest rather than attempting to increase influence, which is not feasible.

How this works for a commercial organisation will depend on its own particular set of stakeholders. In many organisations different stakeholder group relationships are handled by different departments or teams. For instance investors will be handled by Investor Relations (IR), customers by Customer Service, media interest will be handled by Corporate Communications or a dedicated press officer.

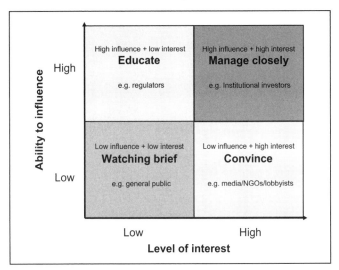

Figure 3.1   A matrix of stakeholder influence and interest

Irrespective of who handles stakeholder communications there is a need to ensure the messages address the fundamental audience needs and expectations. There are at least seven basic communication principles for each of the four stakeholder categories (Figure 3.2).

One final point of note is that most large commercial organisations will have some stakeholder groups for whom there is no designated relationship owner. This, in itself, represents a risk as their needs and expectations may go under-recorded or under-valued. Moreover engagement with these stakeholder groups tends to be reactive not proactive thus putting the organisation in a more vulnerable position in terms of reputation risk.

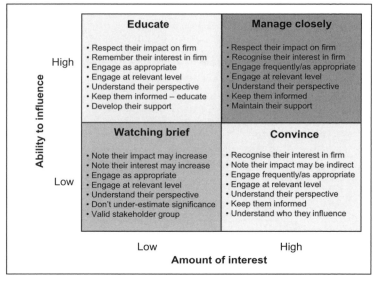

Figure 3.2   The principles of stakeholder communication

Identifying stakeholders is a key requirement of a management team, but allocating relationship owners with clear responsibility is also a duty of good governance. Many large organisations which attract the interest of critical lobby groups tend to adopt a defensive or legalistic approach to them. This is dangerous and counter-productive as some NGOs and political lobbying groups, whilst they may lack direct influence, are capable of influencing the influencers through their contacts with media and politicians. However hostile and irritating these groups may seem they are still stakeholders and require stakeholder management not confrontation.

One final point on stakeholder identification is to note the fluidity of the definition. Stakeholders are self defining issue groups and will come into existence and expire according to the issue. For example, a new site acquisition will engage local planners and residents who have no other claim to stakeholder status beyond the impact in their immediate neighbourhood. The same is true of a divestment or sale of a business unit to a buyer who will cease to be a stakeholder once the transaction is completed. The universe of relevant stakeholders is a moveable feast and is one good reason why stakeholder identification should be part of the cycle of good management practice.

RISK DRIVERS

There is some debate as to whether reputation is a driver or an output and there is a good case for each. As a driver, it has an influence on relationships and thus a good reputation has a positive benefit as an endorser. As an output, a good reputation is the result of operational effectiveness and efficient service delivery. A survey among risk professionals in 2006 found that the majority of senior executives viewed reputation as an output, something that didn't need to be managed providing all operational functions performed as planned.[1] Conversely the risk managers in the survey considered reputation a driver for which senior executives should take more care. In short, each saw reputation as the responsibility of the other, a telling indictment of how the subject is treated in the workplace.

Since the mid 1990s various authors have tried to identify specific drivers of reputation risk and there are a number of different approaches to this. I shall explain four below, although I find that clients like to specify their own list when conducting research. The most famous was created by Charles Fombrun in 1995 for his Reputation Institute in the US. He created a Reputation Quotient (RQ) of 20 attributes across six driver categories (Figure 3.3).

The Reputation Quotient has been refined over the years and it is worth checking the latest ranking system as set out in *Fame and Fortune: How Successful Companies Build Winning Reputations* by Fombrun & Van Riel (2006). The Reputation Quotient gives an aggregate rank score for each corporation in an annual survey. It does not attempt to weight this by stakeholder group. It is possible for an organisation to have a high RQ but still not have a good reputation amongst a key stakeholder group such as investors or customers.

A recent risk analysis for a corporate client used these six categories to identify risk to reputation across each of four primary stakeholder categories: investors, customers, suppliers

---

1   *Strategic Risk* magazine on-line readership survey on Reputation, August 2006 analysed by Chiron.

Category	Attributes
Emotional appeal	How much a company is liked and respected
Products and services	Perceptions of quality, value, innovation and reliability
Financial performance	Competitiveness, profitability, growth prospects and risk
Vision and leadership	Clear vision, strong leadership, initiative
Workplace environment	Management quality, culture, employee quality
Social responsibility	High standards in dealing with people, causes etc

Figure 3.3   Charles Fombrun's Reputation Quotient

and employees. This suggests that the list has resonance today and can be used as a starting point, providing it is tailored to different stakeholder audiences.

A later approach to reputation risk driver analysis came from Dr. Arlo Brady and can be found in his book *The Sustainability Effect – Rethinking Corporate Reputation in the 21st Century* (2005). Dr. Brady identified seven sources of reputation or competitive elements (Figure 3.4).

Further details on these can be found in Chapter 3.5 of his book, but it is a subtly different list from Fombrun's. The Brady categories are designed to help identify the building blocks of a good reputation not to calculate a ranking against peers. The two lists do nevertheless offer a degree of similarity to anyone seeking to put a name to reputation risk drivers.

Category	Attributes
Knowledge and skills	Employee talent pool; drivers of innovation.
Emotional connections	Consumer perception of value; stakeholder alignment
Leadership, vision and desire	Governance style and practice; motivation and vision
Quality	Product or service delivery history; consistency
Financial credibility	History of creating better than average returns
Social credibility	Good citizenship, licence to operate etc.
Environmental credibility	Must not be seen to add negative legacy for future

Figure 3.4   Arlo Brady's categories of risk

There are two other risk driver analyses worth mentioning; one from Henley Management College and one from the Centre for Stakeholding and Sustainable Enterprise (CSSE) at Kingston University.

The Henley model is known as SPIRIT which is an acronym for Stakeholder Performance Indicator, Relationship Improvement Tool.[2] It does what it says, namely provides a tool for improving stakeholder relationships through diagnosing the current state or performance. The Spirit Model looks at 16 attributes across four categories (Figure 3.5).

This risk driver model identifies the relationship quality and indicates where improvement can be made. It highlights the risk where relationship quality is currently poor.

---

2   Henley Management College, School of Reputation and Relationships SPIRIT Model.

Category	Attributes
Past performance	
Experience indicators	7 indicators – service and material benefits, shared values etc
Influence indicators	1 indicator – outside influencers: media, peer, pressure groups
Future performance	
Behaviour indicators	5 indicators – intention to support, recommend or subvert
Emotional indicators	3 indicators – trust and other emotional support indicators

Figure 3.5   The Spirit Model of reputation risk

The final risk driver model is one I developed at Kingston University and is based on the SRI modelling tools used by Morley Asset Management, but with the addition of a predictive or expectation element.[3] Morley score companies based on stewardship and sustainability with one axis 1-5 and one A-E. A company with strong leadership and a sustainable business model will rank A1. The aim of the Kingston model developed by the CSSE is to highlight areas for management attention (Figure 3.6).

This model serves as a strategic planning tool as well an identifier of reputation risk drivers. As reputation risk sits in the gap between company performance and stakeholder expectation any risk model must try to establish a measure of expectation. This is complex but the model recognises the power of attention and association which are highly significant

---

3   Kingston Business School, Centre for Stakeholding and Sustainable Enterprise.

Category	Attributes
Performance	
Stewardship indicators	Board quality, succession planning, decision taking etc
Sustainability indicators	Environmental, social and economic combination
Expectation	
Attention indicators	Media magnetism, generic or specific
Association indicators	Family linkage: corporate or trading brand names

Figure 3.6   The Kingston risk driver model

drivers of reputation risk. Weighting is critical and the model is adaptable not prescriptive.

Risk drivers for reputation risk must focus on a gap analysis between performance and expectation. If the expectation is low there is less risk to reputation by underperformance. Conversely of course, where the expectation is very high then the bar for performance will be equally elevated. Any shortfall represents a risk to reputation. The key is a reliable measure of expectation that does not accidentally influence (raise or lower) it through a survey.

Many organisations undertake regular customer satisfaction or employee feedback surveys, but these are not the same as expectation monitoring. Firstly they are generally conducted to prove or demonstrate adequate levels of satisfaction or empowerment so the purpose of the survey is not to measure but to provide evidence of departmental performance (production, HR and so on). Secondly such surveys are conducted by the company itself and respondents know that this is not an independent enquiry compared to an attitude survey from a research agency.

Identifying stakeholders should be fairly straightforward but identifying risk drivers is more difficult. Most risk departments operate a framework to identify and control risk based on a potential financial impact or cost. Reputation risk is a relationship risk which may have a financial impact but it is rarely immediately apparent, thus it evades scrutiny. As we shall see in succeeding chapters it is more important to determine the tools and controls than to specify risk drivers for this category of strategic risk.

SUMMARY

Stakeholder identification and appreciation is essential for reputation management. Primary stakeholders are vital components of the organisation without whom it would cease to function: investors, employees, customers and suppliers. Secondary stakeholders are no less important but the loss of any one or the addition of a substitute is not business critical.

The drivers of reputation are the metrics by which stakeholders evaluate the organisation and thus determine its value to them. For investors it will be financial performance whereas for employees it will be workplace conditions and opportunities for advancement. Most organisations can identify 6–7 separate drivers of reputation which must be watched closely.

④ Selecting Tools and Controls

The tools and controls for measuring reputation risk are unlike the tools and controls for many other risks. Most risk reporting employs a four box grid or matrix based on the two critical indicators: severity of damage (cost impact) and probability of occurrence (imminent likelihood) (See Figure 4.1). As has already been explained by Nassim Taleb in *Black Swan* a failure to appreciate the low probability risks can be dangerously deceptive.

Reputation risk cannot easily be placed in these boxes. Probability is difficult to predict, relying as it does on the actions, behaviour and performance of the company (that is, its staff and management) to meet stakeholder expectations. Severity of risk is dependent not only on how big the gap actually is between company performance and stakeholder expectation, but also on the speed at which it can be closed. Remember that one very good reason for an absence of insurance cover for reputation is the very real prospect of moral hazard.

The tools for measuring reputation risk require a different currency; probability and severity just won't work. The risk needs to be expressed as a gap of varying size by each stakeholder group. As a starting point, identify the four primary stakeholder groups and show their expectations in relation to seven key risk drivers (see Figure 4.2).

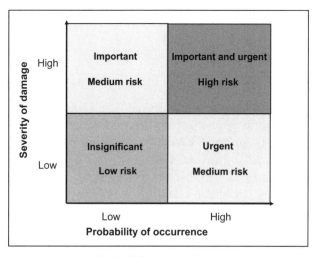

Figure 4.1   A typical risk reporting matrix

The 7 key drivers of reputation	Investors	Customers	Suppliers	Employees
Financial Performance	⊘			
Delivery of Products and Services		⊘	⊘	
Vision and Leadership	⊘			◎
Corporate Responsibility	◎			
Workplace Environment				⊘
Knowledge and Skills	◎	◎		
Emotional Appeal				◎

Figure 4.2   The seven key drivers of reputation

Within this grid you can start to mark up those aspects which are of critical importance to each stakeholder group and which are of less importance to them. It soon becomes clear that failure to 'perform' in key categories represents a higher risk to reputation among certain stakeholder groups compared to others. The dark circles indicate business critical performance areas, that is, 'must have' boxes, whereas the pale circles indicate where performance is expected but less critical, that is, 'nice-to-have' boxes.

This can help focus stakeholder research and ensure that any survey of attitudes probes for expectation in business critical areas for each relevant stakeholder group. For each of the seven reputation determinants there will be subcategories and questions. For example, the employee stakeholder survey may focus on conditions in the workplace and the effectiveness of the management (Figure 4.3).

This approach is for a single stakeholder group on the basis of one set of questions.

A second group worth considering are investors. With the help of the IR department it should be possible to ask investors a set of questions subtly different from those posed to employees, and more appropriate to their concerns and expectations (see Figure 4.4).

From these two examples it is clear that the seven reputation drivers provide a framework for identifying which issues are of particular significance to each stakeholder group. Armed with this knowledge any organisation can judge whether its performance meets, exceeds or falls short of stakeholder expectation for each of its key stakeholder groups. This is the first step towards measuring reputation risk.

EMPLOYEES	Sub-category	Measure stakeholder expectations
Vision and Leadership	Corporate Culture	The organization is open and empowering
	Management Style	Leadership is clear and consistent
	Communication	Goals and targets are explained clearly
Workplace Environment	Engagement	Sense of being part of a team or business unit
	Rewards	Remuneration is market competitive and performance related
	Health and Safety	Workplace is safe and controlled
	Enabling	I am able to do my job effectively with equipment provided
Corporate Responsibility	Appreciation	Management appreciate the workforce as stakeholders
	Ethics	Staff are treated fairly and openly
	Responsibility	My employer cares about environmental impact
	Responsibility	My company is a good corporate citizen
Knowledge and Skills	Expertise	My employer invests in training and development for staff
Financial Performance	Stability	My employer is unlikely to be taken over or cease trading
	Pensions	The pension scheme is sufficient for my retirement
Products and Services	Quality	My employer provides high quality products and services
Emotional Appeal	Employer Brand	My employer cares about the workforce
Knowledge & Skills	Advocacy	I would recommend my employer to others
	Opportunity	There is a clear path for career progression

Figure 4.3   The basis for an employee stakeholder survey

The next step is to compare these expectation surveys among stakeholders with known current and future performance data. It should be possible to spot risk areas and mitigate accordingly. This might mean improving performance or managing expectation downwards. This latter is an art: with investors, analyst briefings are preferable to profit warnings but the overall aim is to avoid surprises which erode confidence and ultimately weaken reputation.

Most companies already have a risk register and sometimes it is worth examining this for relationship risk among specific stakeholder groups. For example, in the grid (Figure 4.5)

INVESTORS	Sub-category	Measure stakeholder expectations
Financial Performance	Profitability	There is evidence of future profitability
	Cash generation/flow	There is evidence of adequate returns to cover pensions etc
	Growth	There is evidence of growth in key business sectors
	Dividend	The return to shareholders is good enough to hold/buy shares
Vision and leadership	Management	There is a strong and well-balanced management team
	Strategy	The business model & strategy for execution are both clear
	Personality	Positive engagement is practised successfully
	Communication	Valuable & actionable, transparent & open
Corporate Responsibility		
	Governance	Evidence of best practice befitting a global business
	Ethics	Evidence of a corporate code and group policy
	Environmental responsibility	Evidence of meaningful activity to address topic
	Social responsibility	Evidence of corporate citizenship
Products and Services	Future-proofing	Products/services address future market needs
	OEM/Services	Evidence of correct balance of business
Workplace Environment	Culture	Evidence that it recruits and retains quality staff
Knowledge and skills	Expertise	Evidence that it has the right skills to service the industry
	R&D	Evidence of investment in innovative technological solutions
Emotional Appeal	Inspiration	Represents a confident & attractive investment

Figure 4.4   The basis for an investor stakeholder group survey

Registered risks	S'holder A	S'holder B	S'holder C	S'holder D	S'holder E
Risk A	★				
Risk B	★				
Risk C	★	★	★	★	★
Risk D	★				
Risk E	★				
Risk F					
Risk G					

Figure 4.5   Risks and their related stakeholder groups

stakeholder group A is affected by all the risks A to E and thus reputation with this group is likely to be critical. In the case of the risk identified as Risk C it appears that this risk is relevant to all stakeholder groups, although much depends on the nature of this risk, it is likely that there is a strong reputational element to it as it impacts so many different stakeholder groups.

This type of analysis is particularly helpful as it builds on information already gathered and assessed by the risk control function.

MONITORING AND TRACKING

So far the discussion on tools and controls to measure reputation risk has focused on the need to identify stakeholder expectation as this is a critical determinant of the risk. The methods outlined earlier in this chapter give examples of how stakeholder attitudes and expectations can be measured according to stakeholder group and reputation driver. This of course may be done by a third party agency as a one-off piece of research, but that will not help set up stakeholder engagement as a management process to reduce risk and eliminate surprises.

In an ideal world each corporate owner of a stakeholder group relationship should have in place a method of monitoring attitude and expectation on a regular basis as an essential part of relationship management. In reality this rarely happens although some groups end up being better understood than others merely due to the frequency of contact. The ideal is to have a company wide tracking system across all stakeholder groups and this acts as a risk control mechanism.

It falls to the owner of each stakeholder group to identify what system will work best for their group and how this can best be integrated into the broader, company-wide, picture of stakeholder expectations. There are, broadly speaking, three key issues, *sampling*, *medium* and *frequency*.

Sampling is a matter of selecting a representative group whose views accurately mirror the vast body of their colleagues within the generic stakeholder group. For customers or employees this is not usually difficult, but for media, regulators and a number of other important stakeholder groups this can be a difficult selection task. I know of several major international corporations where the sheer volume of sub groups whose opinions and attitudes are valid make stakeholder research very difficult to execute. Sample size and composition must be representative and therein lies the challenge for any responsible relationship owner.

Medium is no easier. Some engagement can be by e-mail, some by phone or letter and I know of some organisations who have set up panels of representative stakeholder groups with whom to engage in regular dialogue. If contact is to be by questionnaire then it can be much simpler to do this on-line than on paper. For some stakeholders their opinions must be elicited face-to-face by an interviewer who can probe issues, for others it is possible to use group research such as focus groups. Some types of stakeholder, such as journalists in specialist or trade press, are notoriously reluctant to take part in focus groups.

Frequency depends on the cyclical nature of the business and its reporting timetable. The latter is critical for it is financial results that most typically offer a risk of some surprise or unexpectedly good or poor performance. This is why most IR directors prefer to brief analysts and institutional shareholders regularly to eliminate nasty surprises and manage expectation, even if it is downwards. High frequency engagement is not always appropriate; where legal or regulatory stakeholders are concerned there can be long periods of quiet followed by short periods of intense activity so there is no easy answer for the right or wrong frequency of engagement.

CONTROLS

The aim of any control of reputation risk is to provide an understanding of stakeholder expectations for any given corporate action. In an ideal world the corporation should have a 'finger on the pulse' of its diverse stakeholder groups and know instantly what they expect. Some organisations engage in 'scenario planning' which is an elaborate and sophisticated version of 'what if?' for any given set of events. In my experience there is a best practice methodology as below.

STAGE 1

Set up an attitude survey across all stakeholder groups, both primary and secondary in order to establish a benchmark at a given point in time. This will require working with relationship owners to discuss representative sampling. Use a simple framework such as the seven reputation drivers identified earlier. Determine how often you would want to follow up and verify this information, for example, monthly, half yearly or annually and how best this repeat operation might be conducted, for example, by panel, focus group and so on.

STAGE 2

Ensure that the monitoring of diverse stakeholder attitudes and expectations is recorded and reported to the board frequently. It is important to know how any behaviour or performance will be received. Anticipation is a prudent act of proactive planning. In an evolved management planning cycle the regular feedback from stakeholders can be set against planned performance so that the organisation is audience-aware across all stakeholders and not just investors or customers.

STAGE 3

Reduce and mitigate risk to reputation through positive engagement with stakeholders. Although managing stakeholder relationships and allocating responsibility for risk reduction is the subject of a subsequent chapter, this represents the payback for all the time and effort in setting up a comprehensive stakeholder engagement programme. It is not sufficient to engage only with amenable and affable groups, the frosty and hostile ones must also be included.

RISK REGISTER

It is possible to put reputation risk on the company risk register. Exactly how this is recorded should reflect how easy or difficult it is judged to be to recover trust after an event. Where trust recovery is easy there is low risk and where it is very hard there is high risk. This is not about money or seniority, it is about trust recovery. The approach requires a keen understanding of how the company builds and retains trust among its diverse stakeholder groups.

It is worth revisiting the scale designed for a major UK corporation to enable middle managers to assess where different types of risk to reputation sit within their own spheres of influence (see Figure 4.6).

Risk register

Trust recovery is key to reputation risk classification

Risk impact	Reputation damage profile
Very low	Trust recoverable with little effort or cost – a minor blip on the radar. Risk containable locally – no need to involve senior management, keep informed.
Low	Trust recoverable at modest cost with resource allocation within budgets. Risk containable at sector level – senior management to be kept informed.
Medium	Trust recovery demands cost authorisation above and beyond existing budgets. Risk containable at group sector level – senior management involved.
High	Trust recoverable at considerable cost and management attention. Risk demands immediate attention – dedicated budget and staff.
Very High	Trust severely damaged and full recovery questionable and costly. Risk demands attention of group board and priority action.

Figure 4.6   Degrees of reputation risk

SUMMARY

In order to measure reputation risk it is necessary to appreciate that it is a risk to relationship which means that damage expresses itself in value not cost terms. Attempting to put a financial cost on the risk is frankly a red herring. The risk to reputation sits in the gap between performance (the behaviour or actions of the people within the organisation) and expectation (what stakeholders anticipate based on past actions or stated policy). Measuring reputation risk is therefore an exercise in gap analysis with an emphasis on reducing the gap through managing not only performance but also expectation.

Most risk analyses set out to identify event probability and damage severity as the key determinants, these are not appropriate for reputation risk. Reducing probability to zero is a primary objective of reputation risk management, containing severity is a matter of good corporate communications practice or crisis management. The tools for measuring reputation risk are embedded in good stakeholder engagement where practised by an enlightened management board. Control of the risk can be achieved through heightened responsibility and awareness across the organisation. There are no easy answers or foolproof methods.

(5) Assigning Responsibility

It is ten years since the Turnbull Report on Corporate Governance was published. The report focused on internal control guidance for directors on the combined code, but the most significant recommendation was that major companies should have a system in place for reporting risk. Since then most FTSE 100 companies either have a Chief Risk Officer (CRO) or Risk Committee; some wrap risk reporting within Business Assurance or Internal Audit which are departments that typically report to the Finance Director.

The interpretation of risk will depend on the nature of business and over the last ten years most organisations have become more practised at identifying and reporting operational risk. The majority of risk frameworks set controls in place to identify and mitigate financial impact exposure for their operation. The chart below (Figure 5.1) shows operational risk as applied to the financial services sector. Market risk is also addressed but tends to be used to explain the trading environment in terms of factors beyond control of the company. This will include exchange rates, taxes and shifts in demand which in a poor year give the impression of a list of excuses for under-performance.

Strategic risk is rarely reported and there are two main reasons. Strategic risks cannot be quantified by impact or probability and cannot be assigned to a single individual. They are typically excluded from scrutiny by the risk committee which tends to have an operational function. They should be addressed by the board but too often there is little time or appetite for deep discussion on strategic risk. The second reason is that where strategic risk is acknowledged there can be a reluctance to report it for fear of its value to a competitor or the negative message it might send to investors; strategy is about future direction and any uncertainty must not be expressed outside the boardroom.

The 2006 Companies Act drew on work prepared for the OFR (Operation Financial Review) and introduced a requirement to report on a Principal Risk. This new term appeared to add a fourth category into which Reputation was specifically inserted, despite the fact that it is actually both a principal and strategic risk.

Risk type	Reporting frequency	Control and Predict	Strategy	Examples
Operational Risk	Regularly	Easiest	Retain & manage	**business** – financial, insurance, liquidity, credit, capital, project, ERM, corporate responsibility, brand activity etc.
Market Risk	Occasional	Difficult – no control	Mitigate	**marketplace** – exchange or interest rates, taxation, government policy, competitor activity, pricing, product demand etc.
Strategic Risk	Rarely	Difficult – behavioural	Avoid or Mitigate	**direction** – impact on chosen strategy, sustainability, *reputation*, culture & corporate behaviour, value alignments.
Principal Risk	Statutory requirement	Difficult	Manage	**realisable value** – ROI, significant to investors – share price, *reputation* etc.

Figure 5.1   Types of risk

We shall return to the classification of risk type in a later chapter but it is relevant here because different people in an organisation take responsibility for different types of risk. Few organisations are yet clear about who should be responsible for reputation risk.

CULTURE

Over the past ten years there has been an evolution of risk culture as it becomes clear that more and more business decisions involve some level of risk. At the outset an organisation not only has no risk control capability it also has no perception of the need for one (see Figure 5.2). This is unflatteringly called the unconscious/incompetent or immature stage. As the organisation realises it needs a risk control function it moves to the conscious but still incompetent or adolescent phase.

Once an organisation has a risk control capability it has some competence and is aware of the risks it ought to be controlling. This conscious/competent phase is said to be maturing and

	Conscious	Unconscious
Competent	*Maturing*	*Very mature*
Incompetent	*Adolescent*	*Immature*

Figure 5.2   Stages of risk maturity

it is here where most major corporations sit today. There is a further phase where risk awareness is so embedded in the culture that risk control is automatic or as the model states 'unconscious'. In an ideal world we would all be so risk aware that any risk control department would be superfluous.

Risk has resonance in so many organisations today. In public service safety is critical and the Health and Safety Executive in the UK has grown to prescribe safety in the workplace and identify risk in terms of personal injury. In the construction or manufacturing industries project risk focuses on co-ordinating resources within a time and budget. Risk is expressed in terms of over-run cost and schedule. Risk in the medical world is focused on patient safety. In financial services risk is all about financial loss or exposure to debt.

With regard to reputation I have noticed at least four different levels of maturity from controlled to unmanaged. There are very few at the controlled stage but many at the managed stage and several at the supervised stage, as shown below (Figure 5.3). I do not recommend leaving reputation risk

Control status	Sophistication level	Management process in place to handle risk to corporate reputation
Controlled	Managed by Chief Risk Officer (CRO) **Executive** interest	Reviewed regularly by CFO as a strategic risk and discussed at board level. Supported by independent tracking of diverse stakeholder group attitudes. Sophisticated and sensitive.
Managed	Managed by risk manager (RM). **Operational** interest	Reviewed as part of corporate risk register but not measured or monitored by corporate strategy committee. Compliant with Turnbull guidelines in risk identification but little control over reputation risks.
Supervised	Managed on *ad hoc* basis responsively	Managed on a severity of risk basis by senior management alongside all other operational and strategic risks. Tends to be crisis only, reactive not proactive: fire fighting approach.
Unmanaged	Not managed at all	Reputation risk is not measured or managed in any way – it is not considered a risk worth measuring or trying to manage, other than by having a PR agency to handle any problems if/when they arise.

Figure 5.3   Levels of risk management sophistication

unmanaged but your exact approach depends very much on the nature of your organisation and the type of risks it faces.

APPETITE

Risk is part of our everyday lives, we constantly make decisions about our actions in relation to the rewards offered. For a child, the reward of getting to the sweet shop has to be measured against the risk of crossing the road. Nobody takes risk without an expectation of some reward. Risk appetite depends on role and perspective: an investment banker or city trader reacts differently to a Health and Safety officer or internal auditor. One role is risk hungry, the other risk averse. Risk takers know that high returns require high risk and that low risk will never yield a high return. This *'risk reward ratio'* is understood by all except naïve gamblers.

Reward, as the corollary of risk, comes in many forms. For a bungee jumper the risk of personal injury is weighed against the reward of exhilaration from adrenaline rush. Risk appetite is a personal decision and different individuals exhibit different levels of appetite. In the workplace it has an impact on others so there is commonly a corporate appetite reflecting the nature of the business and how it secures reward and returns. This is most acute in the difference between private and public sector industries.

Sections of the financial services industry specialise in seeking high returns, these have an inherently high appetite for risk. Similarly key players in the fashion industry have a high risk appetite in order to win retailer contracts for their innovative designs. Low appetite for risk taking can be found in public services where there has traditionally been little incentive to take risk for financial gain, as the dangers of risk taking often outweigh any possible rewards.

Appetite for risk is determined by perspective in the role of the individual and in the industry sector, but there is another factor determining risk appetite and that is time. Our appetite for risk shifts according to circumstance and other pressures. A law abiding citizen in secure employment but needing a substantial sum for a life saving operation might find the risk of crime worth taking, especially if the reward, that is, financial gain, outweighed the risk of detection. Irrespective of the moral issues, the risk appetite for this individual is not a fixed value and indicates the susceptibility of risk appetite to circumstance.

Another example of appetite shift occurs in the UK High street where until mid 2007 banks exhibited a relatively high appetite for risk. Expressed through the ease with which customers could secure loans against property, lenders focused more on the asset held as loan security than borrowers' ability to repay. Once banks stopped lending to each other and property values started to decline the appetite for lending swung from high to low, setting off the credit crunch and launching the current recession. While exposure to potential loan defaults continues, UK lenders remain unsure of the full extent of their 'toxic debt'. There is currently a much reduced appetite for risk among lenders compared to a year ago.

How does appetite for risk impact reputation? Many large corporations sponsor sporting and cultural events to gain beneficial media coverage (for example, Volvo sponsors ocean yacht racing and Skandia until recently sponsored Cowes week). Sponsors hope that reputation among their target audience will appreciate through this association. The risk comes with a certain lack of control, for example, a yachting accident might bring the wrong sort of media attention and lead to questions of safety and other negatives. This is a reputation risk: the sponsor weighs the investment decision against possible negative outcomes.

Appetite for risk in the public sector is low because risk is closely linked to personal safety. Most risk assessments done in schools and hospitals focus on the possibility of accident, damage to the people (both public and employees) and insurance liability. Appetite for risk is low because taking risk with personal safety carries too high a cost. This only changes when central government funding cut backs necessitate local initiatives to generate revenue. Once local council services are forced to become profit, as opposed to cost centres, risk to reputation increases. Forced to raise funds locally a council will be obliged to take some risks.

RESPONSIBILITY

Who takes responsibility for corporate reputation in your organisation? The chances are nobody does. In some organisations a charismatic chairman or CEO has their own reputation and this is confused, sometimes deliberately, with that of the corporation. Let's put the question another way: 'who carries the rap when reputation is damaged?' The answer here is the CEO or Board. Investors hold them responsible for protecting and enhancing the reputation as an intangible asset and value driver.

There is a popular misconception that reputation comes under the remit of the Director of Corporate Communications who has both Investor Relations and PR reporting to him. There is no doubt that communications influence reputation but stakeholders are not stupid and they will tolerate only so much spin. Reputation is a reflection of behaviour, actions and performance, whereas communications is about claims, statements and talk. In some organisations there is a significant gap between what they say and what they do. These are often the same organisations with a bad reputation.

I have found plenty of organisations that leave reputation management to the Communications department, however I have never found a Director of Communications willing to take, or capable of taking, responsibility for the organisation's reputation. My experience to date indicates that reputation as a risk gets attention from two key areas in an organisation, one motivated by compliance and the other motivated by control. A highly controversial list of roles and responsibilities tends to open the debate and I present it below to demonstrate how motivation plays a part in who takes responsibility (see Figure 5.4).

Financial and legal compliance are natural attention-getters in any corporate story and reputation risk also appears as a financial asset (intangible) and a corporate liability, neither of which is necessarily fully appreciated by the rest of the board. The compliance motivator is very strong but driven by legislation and specific rules and regulations. The implication is that where not specified it can be omitted. There is little incentive for proactive management.

The Risk and HR functions are also interested in reputation risk but from a control perspective as opposed to compliance. Value cannot be allocated to risk as the impact cost depends partly on how the risk is handled. The HR function should pick up on reputation risk as a corporate reputation depends

Management	Focus	Specifics	Motivation
CEO/Chairman	The City	performance vs peers share price	
Financial Director	Business Review	principal risk asset value description	Compliance
Chief Legal Officer	D&O liability	duty to protect liability for damage	
Risk Director	Governance	control – procedures inclusion within register	Control
Human Resources	Reporting structure	control – people ownership attribution	
Company Secretary	Regulator codes	business community reporting standards	Community
CSR Director	SRI fund managers	stakeholder activism sustainability agenda	
Investor Relations	Investor confidence	analysts briefings shareholdings profile	Choice
Communications	External opinion	public relations media interest	

Figure 5.4   Responsibility and motivation for reputation management

on the action of its employees. Reputation risk is associated with everyone in the organisation not just the people with risk in their job title.

Reputation risk may lie within the remit of the Company Secretary or even CSR Director who can see how the peer group community interpret codes of behaviour, so are well placed. The Company secretary should know what the regulators seek and how competitor reputations compare. The CSR Director will know how the company is performing on sustainability issues and whether the reputation among some external stakeholders needs improving. In both cases these Board members should know how the organisation sits within its business community, what is considered the norm and where the firm sits in relation to it.

The Investor Relations or Communications Directors will be aware of the firm's reputation in terms of comparative appeal and audience choice. They will know that investors and journalists are bombarded by rival firms with information and stories designed to enhance their reputation. More than others they will see reputation as a risk where loss of share of voice or message relevance can cause damage. In only one FTSE100 company to my knowledge is there a dedicated Director of Reputation and he reports to a Director of Corporate Communications.

BEST PRACTICE

There is no ideal title for responsibility for reputation risk, it is actually more important to have the feedback mechanisms in place to sense where the risk exists. A good start is stakeholder engagement survey analysis which should be made available to the Board regularly. The problem with the majority of risk reporting is that it doesn't satisfactorily highlight those decisions required by the board. Many traffic light systems flag up significant risks but lean towards operational not strategic ones, or fail to distinguish between important and urgent.

Each stakeholder group relationship owner should identify where risk to their reputation sits and what damage to it might look like, specifically whether it has a financial impact and how much time and effort would be required to repair the damage and restore trust. From this aggregation of the elements of stakeholder relationship risk a reporting system can be designed. Responsibility should be assigned on the basis of where the greatest source of risk lies.

It is important to remember that having a designated risk owner does not obviate the need for individuals to be vigilant. In some cases, once you allocate a risk manager then the temptation for others is to act as if risk is nothing to do with them. Folly, of course, as a CRO in the public sector claimed in a recent survey:

> *Reputation risk is a consequence of something that happened. This should be recognised as being everyone's risk within the organisation, not just Corporate Communications.*

SUMMARY

The reputation of an organisation is a shared responsibility among all employees, as each is an ambassador in the eyes of non-employee stakeholders. The challenge lies in the control of this responsibility within the management hierarchy. Reputation as a liability takes one owner whereas reputation as an asset takes another. Ownership is frequently inconsistent and therein lies a risk in itself.

The training manual explains the difference between commitment and involvement thus: 'Consider a plate of bacon and eggs, the chicken was involved but the pig was committed'. This is the dilemma for reputation management in a nutshell, how do you get people committed to it while so many are currently involved?

6 Integrating Reputation Risk

Having shown that there is no one accepted owner of reputation risk within an organisation, it must follow that there is no ideal way for the risk to be integrated within a risk control framework. In short as a behavioural risk, reputation protection must be part of the culture of an organisation practised by all employees. Once a role is created with a title of manager or director, there is a tendency for everyone else in the organisation to assume that they therefore have little or no responsibility in that area.

Awareness of the impact on reputation should be an implicit part of any business decision, however sometimes managers get too focused on a process to recognise the bigger picture. Let's take an example outside of business. Guantanamo Bay has undeniably damaged the reputation of the US, as a leader of the democratic world. As an internment and interrogation centre it was deliberately selected to be outside the jurisdiction of US civil law, where only US military law applied. Prisoners were held in legal limbo which the US administration felt appropriate in a post 9/11 world. What would the founding fathers have made of this?

The Obama administration will close down this relict of the Bush era which has done more harm than good for the reputation of the US on the international stage. The UK similarly did itself no favours in pursuing the 42 day detention request. Chosen to allow police to investigate complicated electronic chatter from a number of sources, there was no real excuse for this being much longer than other Western powers. The so called 'war on terror' enabled the state to erode civil liberties and thus devalue the reputation of a once revered legal system. Reputation damage was an acceptable cost in the eyes of the politicians. This is a reminder that reputation is a composite of actions which in themselves seem acceptable but, taken collectively, accidentally cause harm to a core value. Remember, nobody sets out to damage reputation.

Returning to the corporate stage, how then do you ensure that reputation risk is controlled? It doesn't have the same reporting metrics as many operational risks and the scale of risk is open to interpretation until it is too late. How does a significant risk get the attention it deserves, based on its possibility as opposed to probability? The answer is really to stop thinking defensively about protection, which puts you on the back foot, and start thinking about leverage and enhancement, which calls for a constructive, offensive strategy of reputation building. This is the one great advantage of reputation risk being handled outside the risk department, the correct strategy is not about control but exploitation. The best form of defence is attack.

ALTERNATIVE APPROACHES

There are four basic approaches to integrating reputation risk. Which one is right for you depends on the nature of your organisation. Certain approaches may require too great a level of cultural change and will be unworkable in some environments. Others are more suitable for the public or retail sectors where there is a high level of customer interface and where reputation risk is most obviously present.

1. Board review

Reputation risk is identified and discussed at monthly board meetings so that action can be taken as appropriate. This requires stakeholder feedback to be recognised as an essential part of the strategic planning process. It also requires that members of the Board act as representatives for each stakeholder interest group and can confidently claim to understand their expectations. For this to work, board members need to be educated in the principles of reputation risk.

Many boards review the risk register on a regular basis but rely on traffic light coding to identify the most actionable risks, which are usually those with the highest cost potential. Reputation does not comfortably fit these metrics so a more relevant flagging system will need to be used and here it is up to the strategy, communications and risk directors to work out an appropriate system.

The advantages of this approach are that it is handled at the top of the organisation from where corporate culture should emanate. Awareness of reputation risk should therefore permeate the organisation. The disadvantages of this approach can be an absence of individual responsibility and a tendency for some boards to regard risk reporting as in itself boring and perfunctory. Strategic risks need to be given time for discussion and should be driven by those responsible for strategy as much as for risk if the subject is to be taken seriously. Strategic risk is not a mandatory reporting category, thus it tends to be a discretionary activity with less management time than it deserves.

2. Risk department

    The Risk department is considered a natural home for any threat to business continuity or performance cost. The remits of many risk committees or risk officers deal primarily with tangible or measurable risks, certainly the operational risks and sometimes the market ones. In many organisations the role of the risk function is to report danger to the board. This rarely includes strategic risk, inherent in doing business.

    The greatest danger when integrating reputation within other risk reporting lies in the difficulty of recognising and articulating it in a meaningful way. Theoretically it should be possible to add strategic risks to operational and market ones so that risk reporting is comprehensive, however some risks cannot be seen within the organisation and require an independent viewpoint. Even if expressed and categorised there is then a problem of selecting the appropriate handling strategy and individual responsibility for control.

    Reputation risk is probably too much of a holistic concept to be reported reliably by a risk officer or committee. In some cases it can be a matter of diplomacy. For example, a chairman or CEO who is known to enjoy giving press briefings without the press officer present represents a reputation risk, but who would mention this outside the boardroom?

3. HR department

As a behavioural risk, reputation risk is inherent in all activity by staff, so the more staff an organisation employs the greater the reputation risk. For a public service operator like BA or the BBC it only takes one member of staff to upset a customer for the whole organisation to suffer a risk to reputation. There is therefore a very good case for reputation risk to be managed by the HR department as an implicit element of staff training. For major retailers and customer service operators, the role of staff as ambassadors of the firm is ingrained from the outset.

The vulnerability of reputation and its risk exposure should be assessed by the board in relation to the nature of the business in which they operate. Staff training in reputation risk awareness can only be effective if management fully appreciate the significance of employee actions in both protecting and endangering corporate reputation. The causal links in the chain from action to reputation impact must be fully understood.

4. Communications

In many organisations the role of reputation protection is left to Corporate Communications (internal and external) in the belief that publicity will create a positive impression and thus protect reputation. In most cases the Communications department can only control the output of broadcast messages, it cannot control the corporate behaviour or culture on which reputation depends. Corporate Affairs, Investor Relations and PR (in-house or agency) all play a role in communication of corporate messages but stakeholders make up their minds based on a variety of information feeds.

An organisation might produce an ethics policy explaining how it practices good corporate governance, treats suppliers, customers and staff fairly, sources sustainable material, or is carbon neutral. If the reality of the business is different then stakeholders may see a gap between what the organisation says and what it does. This gap erodes trust and damages reputation.

HOLISTIC APPROACH

The correct approach to reputation risk is to remember that reputation is relational and specific. Your organisation has a relationship with someone (a stakeholder) for something (a differentiating aspect). Only by returning to the basic analysis of this can risk control (protection or enhancement) be effective. Here are some examples by industry sector.

MANUFACTURER

A manufacturer has a reputation for producing high quality products, these justify a premium price because they are well made and durable. They perform their function admirably and thus deliver value for money to customers with whom the firm enjoys a good reputation. What then would reputation risk look like? What would damage this reputation? The answer is a perceived drop in quality reducing the value perception held by customers. Two things can cause this: reduction in quality by this firm or significantly higher quality offered by a rival firm.

A reputation *protection* strategy might ensure quality control standards are maintained but this assumes customer expectations are not influenced by external factors such as new competition. Customers make their judgements of value based on choice in the marketplace at the time of purchase. By contrast a reputation *enhancement* strategy would aim not for high quality products but highest quality, a subtle but significant difference indicating a greater degree of competitor awareness.

RETAILER

A retailer has a reputation for stocking a comprehensive range of goods in a particular category. They have a reputation not only for holding the goods but also delivering within seven days. Customers are prepared to pay a slight premium for this efficient and reliable service. What would reputation risk look like? What would damage this reputation? The answer is a failure to supply goods or provide them within seven days. The reputation is built on reliability to supply and it is this on which customers depend. As with the manufacturer, two things can damage their reputation: one is simply a failure to supply on time and the other is competitors offering even quicker delivery.

A reputation *protection* strategy will focus on maintaining the promised delivery timetable, however a reputation *enhancement* strategy will focus on exceeding customer expectation and delivering in under a week. As in the case of the manufacturer this is a simplified and one-dimensional example; customer expectations will cover other criteria and not just product quality or delivery time. But it is sufficient to show the basic difference between protecting reputation from risk and enhancing it to remove risk.

PROFESSIONAL FIRM

A local firm of solicitors enjoys a reputation for handling property transactions efficiently for their clients. Within the town they are respected by estate agents, surveyors and banks as a particularly professional partnership. With each new instruction comes the pressure to maintain the good reputation and so standards are rigorously upheld. What would reputation risk look like? What could cause them damage? Any sale or purchase contract which takes longer or costs more than the client expected has the potential to damage the firm's reputation.

A reputation *protection* strategy will be implicit in the firm's operational handling of the transaction and the correct drafting and exchange of relevant legal paperwork. The quality of its people and processes will be monitored by not only the client partner but probably an overview partner to assess compliance and client satisfaction. A reputation *enhancement* strategy will go beyond internal system control and look to manage the client expectations throughout the engagement, not simply relying on the review at completion. A business that is based on client (or customer) satisfaction must put in place a monitoring system to identify client satisfaction issues throughout the relationship.

PUBLIC SECTOR

A local council enjoys a reputation for managing its finances prudently and in such a way that it can keep council tax charges relatively low, despite reduced contributions from central government. Residents appreciate this efficient management of public service and thus the council enjoys a reputation for sound fiscal management. What would reputation risk look like? What would damage this reputation? Evidently any significant rise in council tax charges.

A reputation *protection* policy will aim to exploit the fiscal prudence of the council and this may or may not become a feature of local election politics. A reputation *enhancement* strategy will aim to manage taxpayer expectations through demonstrating careful and considered allocation of council spending across public services (both directly and indirectly controlled). In this way the public increase their understanding of the council priorities and are more sympathetic towards future increases in charges. The mantra of no surprises is thus practised as a key element of reputation risk control.

SUMMARY

There is no simple way to manage reputation risk. The aim is to prevent a situation in which reputation damage can occur, and thus protection might seem the best policy. As we have shown a reputation is earned with a stakeholder group for a specific attribute, so the key is to understand what this is and with whom it matters. This will help identify a protection strategy but in itself this may not be enough as external factors influence stakeholder expectations.

It is not enough merely to improve performance by 20 per cent year on year if the market sector in which you operate is growing by 30 per cent. You will inevitably lose ground to competitors. Integrating reputation risk cannot merely be concerned with internal controls, it must by necessity incorporate external factors such as competitor activity and the marketplace environment, which affect stakeholder expectations. Risk to reputation sits in the gap between performance and expectation (see Figure 6.1).

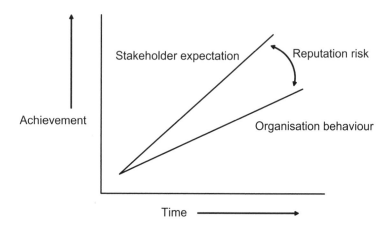

Figure 6.1   The reputation risk gap

⑦ Governance and Compliance

Moving on from measuring and managing risk we come to reporting. Ever since the Turnbull report on good governance it has been accepted among leading public companies that risk should be reported. But why does anyone report risk let alone reputation risk? The simple answer is that shareholders and regulators expect reassurance that value damaging possibilities have been identified and as far as possible neutralised. The main purpose of reporting risk has thus focused implicitly on risk as threat not risk as opportunity. Risk reporting has, to date, been about value protection not value enhancement. The inherent risks that businesses must take to generate wealth and increase value are rarely reported as risk.

The two most important questions surrounding risk reporting are: what exactly should be reported and to whom? The audience is, of course, critical as different stakeholders will perceive risk differently. A risk to an employee or customer will be different to a risk to an investor or regulator. The Accounting Standards Board (ASB) specifies the content of the company Annual Report and the primary audience is deemed to be shareholders (current and prospective) who are termed 'members'. With this audience in mind risk reporting must inspire confidence and demonstrate a sound return on investment free from uncertainty or risk (see Figure 7.1).

Risk type	Reporting frequency	Control and Predict	Strategy	Examples
Operational Risk	Regularly	Easiest	Retain & manage	**business** – financial, insurance, liquidity, credit, capital, project, ERM, corporate responsibility, brand activity etc.
Market Risk	Occasional	Difficult – no control	Mitigate	**marketplace** – exchange or interest rates, taxation, government policy, competitor activity, pricing, product demand etc.
Strategic Risk	Rarely	Difficult – behavioural	Avoid or Mitigate	**direction** – impact on chosen strategy, sustainability, *reputation*, culture & corporate behaviour, value alignments.
Principal Risk	Statutory requirement	Difficult	Manage	**realisable value** – ROI, significant to investors – share price, *reputation* etc.

Figure 7.1   Risk reporting

A regulator expects risk reporting to display a thorough and comprehensive examination of possible damage to value as evidence of good and competent governance. The regulator will only be satisfied if procedures at or close to 'best practice' are in place and employed. The Companies Act 2006 requires the Business Review (clause 417, paragraph 3) to contain 'a description of principal risks and uncertainties facing the company' which include of course reputation as this affects value. The regulator or law maker will have a different view on risk reporting to the investor as their needs are different. The regulator is concerned with trust in the system whereas the investor is only concerned with trust in his own investment.

A recent comparative study of annual report content among the top UK banks and insurers[1] found a high level of detail in *operational risk* as one might expect given the nature of the business. The level of detail on *market risk* was likewise quite thorough given the importance of external factors to financial performance of individual companies. A cynic might note that a typical chairman's report will cite market forces as the primary cause for under performance in order to divert attention from management failings. The level of detail on *strategic risk* was, by contrast, very poor indeed indicating either a failure to recognise it or a reluctance to reveal it.

The Accounting Standards Board does not venture a definition of *principal risk* so it is open to interpretation by each individual report publisher. The study concluded however that principal risk should relate to realisable value for it to have a meaning among investors in a publicly quoted company. Why then such poor reporting of strategic and principal risk? Is it perhaps because they are each harder to predict and control than operational risk, or is it because they have some commercial sensitivity, revealing weaknesses for competitors to exploit?

RISK AND STRATEGY

FutureValue is an agency that specialises in examining company reports to determine the added value offered to investors by the copy content as distinct from the figures and charts. The MD of the agency, Ian McDonald Wood has a view on why report content is so uniformly uninformative to those who seek to understand the balance of strengths and weaknesses:

---

1   FutureValue, strategic value audits in Financial Services www.futurevalue.co.uk.

Many companies are reluctant to talk about their risks in the annual report, especially strategic risks. Fear of revealing information valuable to competitors or destroying investor confidence leaves the impression that the risks have not been recognised.

Investors are more interested in the strategies in place for handling identified risks than the magnitude or nature of the risks themselves. They are seeking assurances that the management team is competent to deal with risk, not that risk has been eliminated.

– Ian McDonald Wood.

This is important as companies rarely identify the strategies for handling risk because they often fail to categorise risk correctly. Some risk must be managed and cannot be eradicated – it can be reduced or mitigated but it will always be present, avoidance is not an option. Reputation risk is a risk that must be managed so any reporting of it must surely talk of how this is done. It is patently insufficient to say that 'Our reputation is very important to us and highly valued' without saying how the risk is managed, although several reports do just this.

Another weakness in risk reporting is the focus on process of risk handling at the expense of the nature of risk which is often ignored:

Companies rarely report risk factors as potential perils that impact upon future performance. There is often a disconnect between evaluation of the risk factors and the strategic direction of the organization.

It is as though one has nothing to do with the other. Risk is seen as part of governance and not strategy ... best practice is for the risk management process *to be part of governance reporting while the* risk factors *themselves should be an integral part of the strategy reporting.*

– Ian McDonald Wood.

This is a very significant point, risk reporting is almost universally about processes and controls which demonstrate an ability to protect company value. Risk reporting hardly ever mentions the nature of the risks themselves as this is rarely considered relevant to the report author, although it may have been covered in discussions at the risk or audit committee. Risk as governance has a narrow focus and it is common for the strategy section of a company report to omit any mention of risk, either as threat or opportunity.

As a result of the above I offer the following seven points as part of a checklist for risk reporting, as a precursor to talking about reputation or any other strategic risk. I think it is very important for both the Risk and Strategy departments to talk freely about risk, one talking about processes and one about factors. This approach is helpful to anyone tasked with reporting risk in their organisation:

1. Explain whether the risk represents a threat, opportunity or uncertainty.

2. Explain taxonomy or classification of risk, for example, market, strategic and operational.

3. State strategies for dealing with identified risk, for example, avoid, mitigate, manage.

4. For governance explain systems and controls of risk handling process.

5. For strategy explain risk factors and issues in respect of their future impact.

6. Explain what you mean by principal risk.

7. Talking about risk is not a sign of weakness. However, failure to show how risk will be handled certainly is a weakness.

PERFORMANCE AND RISK MANAGEMENT

Risk management as a discipline is broadening into Enterprise Wide Risk Management (EWRM) and the big question is how to reconcile risk control with business performance. There are three major drivers for compliance in this marketplace that are related to specific industries along with a fourth, generic driver:

Industry	Driver
Public Sector	The Orange Book http://www.hm-treasury.gov.uk/risk_guidance.htm
Banking	Basel II http://www.fsa.gov.uk/Pages/About/What/Inter-national/basel

Insurance	Solvency II http://www.fsa.gov.uk/pages/About/What/Inter-national/solvency
General business	BS 31000 http://www.itgovernance.co.uk/products/2030 or http://www.standardsuk.com

THE ORANGE BOOK

Although first published by the Treasury in 2004, The Orange Book is still a very good introduction to risk for anyone operating in the public sector. It sets out how to interpret and identify risk in terms of public service provision. Good governance is expressed in terms of sound judgement in the appropriation and allocation of public funds. The Office of Government Commerce (OGC) first published guidance on risk in 2002 when private funding for public sector projects (PPE) was a concern. This enabled a distinction to be made between business and project risk.

BASEL II

Basel II is a regulatory framework for the Banking industry. The aim is to integrate risk management within business performance; in a sense moving risk maturity from adolescent to adulthood. Risk will ultimately be seen less as a separate discipline than integral to corporate thinking and future performance as part of a more risk aware culture. Basel II is about evolving towards an integrated platform to allow greater efficiency and reduce cost.

SOLVENCY II

This is a European regulatory framework directive for the Insurance industry and concerns itself with the risk firms run in respect of their capital requirements. In short it is about risk tolerance and aims to answer the key question: 'How much risk can we afford to take?' As the accountancy firm KPMG states in its own briefing on the directive (KPMG Survey Briefing, Edition No. 3, December 2007):

> *The industry has been given its biggest opportunity for decades to assist in the development of the new regime and create a truly competitive European-wide market where each organisation can demonstrate its capital strength as well as give a fair account of its past activities. It is proposed that Solvency II will be a risk-based economic framework which gives insurers an incentive to measure and monitor their risks and have their capital requirements determined by this risk assessment.*

The same paper notes that reputation is a key strategic asset for any insurance firm:

> *Reputation is a key success factor for any insurance company. Corporate reputation produces trust, the amount and quality of which generally is one of the most influential variables for the behaviour of internal and external stakeholders: customers' inclination to sign a contract, investors' readiness to provide capital, journalists' willingness to provide positive coverage to the public and the favourable behaviour of any other stakeholder. All these factors critically depend on the respective stakeholder's trust and benevolence*

which are substantially rooted in a strong and positive corporate reputation.

BS 31100

Launched in October 2008 this is a new British Standard on risk management based on the new International ISO 31000 standard. According to the BSI website:

BS 31100 establishes the principles and terminology for risk management. It also gives recommendations for the model, framework, process and implementation of risk management gained from experience and good practice. It should be used for:

- *Ensuring that your business achieves its objectives.*
- *Ensuring risks are proactively managed in specific areas or activities.*
- *Overseeing risk management in your company*
- *Providing assurance on your risk management strategy.*
- *Reporting to stakeholders, for example, through annual financial statements, corporate governance reports or corporate social responsibility reports.*

This key standard for risk management is useful to CEOs, CFOs, CROs, CIOs, COOs and CTOs; chairmen and company secretaries; managing, IT and finance directors; risk, insurance, claims and business continuity managers; information security specialists; underwriters; Health and Safety officers; and heads of legal affairs.

BEST PRACTICE

Reporting reputation risk is in its infancy, and even those corporations where reputation is recognised as a valuable asset, generally fail to report on how this is protected in risk terms. There is of course no shame in reporting that a good reputation is only an asset if its value can be protected or enhanced. The better a reputation the more harmful will be any damage, thus being more vulnerable, the greater the risk to value. Reporting reputation risk should therefore be an act of assurance not an admission of weakness. What then would a good risk report look like for reputation risk?

Best practice reporting will show that the organisation understands its stakeholders well enough to prevent any failure to meet their expectations. This understanding will be evidenced through good measurement, and ultimately good management, of the risk. The three key constituents of effective and confidence-inspiring reporting of reputation contain these three elements.

1. Understanding

    a) **Stakeholders** – Demonstrate that all stakeholder groups are recognised and appreciated. Many organisations still do not acknowledge the diversity of stakeholder interests or their significance. It should be a fundamental requirement of all stakeholder relationship owners to understand why their relationship group or interface is a stakeholder, how their interests manifest in terms of impact upon the organisation or how the organisation impacts upon them. If you don't know why someone is a stakeholder then you fall at the first hurdle. Remember one cynical definition of a stakeholder as *'anybody who can bugger up your business'*.

b) **Reputation** – How many organisations actually understand the building blocks of their reputation, which stakeholder relationships are critical and what values make them so in the absence of a Director of Reputation who actually takes this on? It falls between Marketing and Communications and sometimes is of interest to the CEO, but it usually lacks a dedicated owner or sponsor. Stakeholder awareness, or lack of it, is often the reason. Understand the different relationships and you understand the building blocks of reputation. It is then possible to see where value and its corollary, potential damage, both lie.

c) **Risk** – Once reputation is understood and expressed as an asset then risk to the value of this asset should be self-evident. Risk to reputation should be expressed as not only threat but also opportunity, but any uncertainty about a relationship with stakeholders represents a risk. Scenario Planning or 'What if?' analysis can help to plot where and how damage might occur. One thing is for sure, it is not possible to express the risk without an understanding of the stakeholder relationships and the quality of reputation that exists with each group.

2. Measurement

Apart from regular dialogue with stakeholders in order to understand their expectations and ensure effective delivery of the no surprises philosophy, it is important to conduct attitude surveys regularly. Frequency will depend on the nature of the organisation and the speed of change within the business environment; most organisations do annual surveys some do them every quarter. Conducting the survey is only half the job, the other half is responding to it. Ideally stakeholder feedback data should be fed directly into the strategic planning process, sadly in some organisations it sits in the research department awaiting analysis until too late.

Measuring reputation and measuring risk are not the same but as previously explained you cannot measure risk to reputation until you have agreed how you measure reputation. Measuring reputation risk is a gap analysis taking stakeholder expectation and organisation performance as the two variables. The aim is to narrow or close the gap in order to reduce the risk. This is done by influencing stakeholder expectation, or adjusting organisation performance, or ideally a subtle combination of both.

3. Management

Reputation risk is carried by everyone in the organisation from the shop floor to the boardroom, so the sooner your culture reflects this, then the better equipped it is for handing the risk. Reporting how the risk is managed is important to investors and regulators so it is insufficient to talk merely of processes and controls. It will be necessary to demonstrate how employees create and enhance your reputation through their actions rather than the restrictions on trying to protect it. This is essential in service industries where customer or client service is an integral part of reputation.

SUMMARY

Governance and compliance is only partly about knowing the latest reporting rules about disclosure or transparency, it is also about understanding why reporting is done. Reporting should be done to inform and inspire, to spread confidence in leadership of the organisation. Awareness of reputation should be an essential part of this as a good reputation inspires confidence and attracts investors, employees and customers.

Many corporate reports are treated as a chore, pored over by the legal team to edit sensitive information to the bare minimum required by the regulator. The purpose of the OFR (Operating and Financial Review), which was absorbed into the 2006 Companies Act, was to increase the amount of information in the public domain and improve transparency. Reporting should be seen as an opportunity to compete for investors rather than as a compliance document. Reputation risk reporting provides an opportunity to talk about strategic risk as a topic of competitive advantage and certainly not as an uncontrolled threat to value.

⑧ Case Studies

PUBLIC SECTOR

Many public sector operators have greater exposure to reputation risk than private sector corporations. This is because expectations held by the stakeholder group labelled 'general public' cover such a vast range of qualities that the risk of failing to meet them is higher. The three case study examples shown cover national and local government plus a public service broadcast corporation. In each case reputation damage is expressed as an erosion of trust rather than immediate financial cost.

There is also a political element absent from most reputation risk in the private sector. Any failures in public service delivery offer political capital to opposition politicians and media, who readily take an opportunity to claim they would act differently. Everyone thinks they would spend public money better than the incumbent administration and every reputational 'knock' incident provides a platform to enhance your party's reputation at the expense of the hapless incumbent party. Delivering an effective public service, deploying money from taxpayers, leaves any administration open to criticism.

Stakeholders in public services tend to be more vocal because they have contributed financially (via their taxes) and this gives them a right to complain. Complaints invariably make good news stories so incidents attract media interest. The result is that only good news stays local, bad news travels far and wide ... fast. Reputation risk in public service therefore 'comes with the territory' and is inherent. This does not mean that it need not be mitigated, the key question in the public sector remains trust erosion: 'How much trust can we afford to lose before it cannot be regained?' Moreover, 'What happens when trust is lost?'

1.1 IDENTITY & PASSPORT SERVICE (IPS) – HOME OFFICE

Background

The IPS is a department of the Home Office responsible for issuing passports for UK citizens. It will also be responsible for introducing Identity Cards in the near future, about which there is much public scepticism. This has not yet been debated by parliament, but the scheme is known to be costly and there is some doubt as to whether the benefits fully outweigh the cost. Security experts and broadsheet journalists remain unconvinced by the government rationale for these cards, yet the IPS is pushing ahead in the hope of winning public support over the long term. Several recent losses of public records by government agencies have not inspired the public. There is suspicion both for the motives in collection and the competence in handling of personal data required by the identity card system.

The UK Border Agency (UKBA) is another Home Office department responsible for issuing identity cards to foreign UK residents who are not UK citizens, and this agency has already begun to introduce identity cards among a minority group with little power to resist. Knowing the attitude of the

UK public the IPS has been tasked with introducing cards to key groups favourably disposed to the cards. However airline pilots, among supposedly willing citizen groups, have signalled a reluctance to act as guinea pigs in the low key launch. Action groups like No2ID are marshalling support to resist the cards, despite the clear intention of the government to brush aside resistance in the name of state security.

Since the UK opted out of the Schengen agreement with the rest of the EU in 1990, all UK citizens must use passports at international border crossings, where EU citizens need only Identity Cards. Many feel the UK government motivation is nothing to do with falling in line with Schengen and more to do with state security and the 'war on terror'. The British public are very suspicious of identity cards which reflect a policy to amass and store personal data at the expense of civil liberties.

Reputation – What is at Risk?

The reputation of the Home Office, and thus the government, with the general public is at risk through pursuing a policy known to have widespread resistance. Is unpopularity itself a risk? Yes, if diminished public trust results in ejection of the political party in government. Any democratic government needs to retain public support to endorse its mandate to govern however, it knows it cannot please all its citizens equally.

The main risk comes from the political capital this hands an opposition party. The full expense has yet to be put before parliament and the cost-benefit debated in the House. It is highly likely that there will be claims taken up in the media that this is a waste of taxpayers' money, and that the budget could be better deployed in other areas of state expenditure such as schools and hospitals.

Apart from the general public there is a reputation risk among key groups such as security experts and law enforcers. Very few security experts support the introduction of identity cards and will think less of the government for ignoring their advice. Similarly the reputation of the government among its own law enforcement agencies will not be improved through adding to the burden of their workload.

International stakeholders will be surprised that having shunned Schengen the UK government now wants to introduce identity cards to run in parallel with passports. Many foreign governments will see this belt and braces policy as indulgent and unnecessary, however the reputation of the Home Office outside the UK is perhaps less significant than that of the Foreign Office.

There is one area where reputation will be improved and that is with the consultancies and card producers tasked with introducing the scheme. These approved suppliers will gain financially from government contracts and thus, in their eyes, the Home Office will have a reputation as a good customer.

Risk Mitigation

How then could this risk to reputation be reduced? Clearly a great degree of for public support would reduce the risk. To date there has been no attempt to win over public opinion on the benefit of carrying identity cards. There is no apparent advantage to the individual only, a vague benefit to state security. From a commercial perspective it would first be necessary to encourage people to want a card and see some benefit in carrying it.

During 2008 a number of embarrassing data loss incidents by government departments and agencies reduced public trust in the ability of the government to keep confidential records secure. Little has since been done to convince the public that the government is a responsible custodian of a mass of personal data. This is a separate but relevant condition for greater public support of identity cards.

The current strategy for winning over the public appears to be based on winning over sections of the public in turn to create a momentum. The first phase of 'low resisters' is thought to include airline workers, although even they have indicated some resistance. Even if a 'guinea pig' group can be found there is no evidence that wider approval is guaranteed. At the time of writing the IPS is recruiting a Head of Communications who presumably will pick up the brief to win over the public.

Among sceptics there is a belief that the government will soon tire of trying to encourage people to adopt the system and make card carrying compulsory for all UK citizens. In the early stages incentives will probably be linked to benefit support from the Department of Work and Pensions or tax credits from HM Revenue and Customs, but ultimately the system will become mandatory. Reputation risk mitigation depends on finding and communicating a benefit to the card holder so that people willingly carry the card.

1.2 HAMPSHIRE COUNTY COUNCIL

Background

Hampshire County Council is one of the first county councils to place reputation on their corporate risk register. There are two main drivers. The first is the changing landscape of reporting demanded by the Audit Commission, switching from council performance metrics under the CPA to wider assessment to include stakeholder relationship effectiveness under the new CAA. The second is the appreciation of what damage can arise as evidenced by local authorities where failure in social services (child protection) severely reduces trust both from central government and the public.

There are other factors in the political landscape operating as well. The government is keen for the public to have greater choice in service provider and there is a move towards personalisation in adult and child services provided by the county council. This brings reputation into focus as does the trend to prove value for money to a national government keen to create more unitary authorities (usually urban conglomerates) at the expense of county boundaries thus removing vital revenue in the form of taxpayers. The county council needs to prove its value, and thus its raison d'etre, to both the public and the government.

Despite balancing a budget where demand for services regularly outstrips the supply of funds, the county council recognised that some services offer greater potential to generate revenue than others. There is a close correlation between the appetite for risk and the commercial potential of individual services. As a result a risk matrix was developed to plot the council's appetite for risk with specific regard to reputation damage potential (see Figure 8.1). For example, a failure in child protection services would be highly damaging but a failure in parks and amenities would be less damaging. This approach enabled the county council to address reputation risk in a way that reflected the relationship between risk appetite and impact damage. It also helped show which services should be viewed as cost centres as opposed to profit centres.

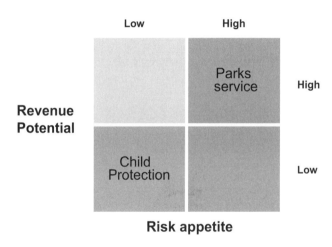

Figure 8.1   Revenue potential and risk appetite

Reputation – What Risk?

With whom does the county council need a good reputation? There are many diverse stakeholder groups to consider. The public as customers of its services but also central government and regulators (for example, Audit Commission) both of whom play a significant part. Suppliers and contractors are also significant for they fulfil much of the council's public service duties, so they expect to be well briefed and remunerated. The media is of course an important opinion former and many councils are concerned to get good rather than bad coverage for their activities.

It was suggested by Michael Power in the Demos paper 'The Risk Management of Everything' that the political nature of local government means that reputation is a secondary risk, a consequence of actions with an impact on legitimacy to control public funds:

> *The growing enfranchisement of publics and stakeholders in risk regulation regimes has much to do with managing the perceived legitimacy of regulatory activity and decisions. There is more than a hint that risk communication strategies are as concerned with managing the secondary or reputational risk to regulators, public bodies and government as they are about the primary risk that is to be regulated.*

In public service the primary risk is the operational risk of failing to deliver a service, but the secondary risk is that to legitimacy in the eyes of the public and whether it is considered 'fit for purpose'. In local government there are the elected members who have a short term tenure working alongside civil servants who are employed irrespective of the political party in power. Each body has the capacity to damage the reputation of the council through its actions, remember some seek shorter term solutions (that is, quick wins) than others.

The risk to reputation in the case of this county council necessitates the appetite for risk to be measured across each of the different departments to assess what is in effect risk tolerance. Some services will draw media and regulator censure more readily than others and thus offer a higher reputation risk. For example, any shortfall in child or adult care provision versus expectation will gain adverse media attention.

This council is concerned about media coverage. Some stories in the local press or regional TV are small and do no lasting damage, but other stories gain national attention and last for weeks. Newsworthiness is relative and a story meriting broadcast one day can be dumped the next due to a higher priority item. Once a story reaches a certain critical momentum only sackings or resignations may be sufficient to draw a line under the incident.

Risk Mitigation

How do you mitigate the risk of acquiring a poor reputation? Quite simply, through aiming to have a good reputation, based on what you know is expected of you. It is important to understand what the public expect, for example, if you reduce rubbish collection to fortnightly from weekly it is not enough to say that other councils are doing the same, especially if your public still expect weekly collections. Risk mitigation requires matching performance with expectations. Where those expectations are too high or 'unreasonable' then managing them downwards is an essential part of the risk mitigation strategy.

The key in media handling is of course to reduce the *newsworthiness* of any potentially harmful story. While this in part depends on the relative newsworthiness of other stories it can be controlled through effective media handling by a skilled press officer. Many councils now ensure that their spokesmen undergo training, however an investigative journalist will always find an uncensored source if they feel they are being manipulated or kept from the truth.

The long term mitigation strategy is to create a culture where consequences of specific actions are well understood. Reputation protection becomes the duty of all council employees. The provision of social services is a very difficult field in which to exceed 'customer' expectations, it is much easier to fail to meet expectations and disappoint. Knowing this of course becomes part of the strategy to mitigate reputation risk, managing not only performance but also expectation.

1.3 THE BBC

Background

The BBC is a public service broadcaster funded partly from the TV licence fee from householders and partly from its own enterprise division. The licence fee is of course reviewed by the government and is theirs to increase, reduce or remove as they see fit. Following the Hutton enquiry when both the Director General Greg Dyke and Chairman Gavyn Davies were forced to leave, the corporation has been regulated jointly by the Trustees and Ofcom. The memorandum of understanding between them was signed only in July 2008, yet in October a broadcast on Radio 2 Russell Brand show attracted 42,000 complaints.

The right-wing press led by the *Sunday Mail* whipped up a campaign against the BBC and within weeks the issue had moved from one isolated offensive broadcast through the inadequacies of editorial control procedures to ultimately questioning the salaries of BBC executives which seemed high in relation to their capabilities. Ultimately the issue gravitated to BBC accountability: how licence fee revenue was spent and whether the corporation delivered value for money. The Director General, Mark Thompson, had to quickly reassure the government that his corporation was indeed well managed and that the licence fee was being well invested. In the course of the scandal which became known as 'Sachsgate' some heads did roll but the incident shone a light on the culture of the BBC and how much this has changed in the technological age.

Many BBC programmes are produced under contract and provided by independent companies, often run by the presenter who is the ratings draw, for example, Russell Brand or Jonathan Ross. The BBC accept this commercial arrangement despite being aware of the risk exposed by previous controversial or 'edgy' presenters such as Chris Evans. The BBC programme controllers compete for audience ratings in a highly competitive broadcast environment and their belief is that presenters win audiences, especially youth audiences. The editorial culture prior to Sachsgate was not in favour of censorship unless absolutely necessary and this represented a high risk, especially to a conservative Middle England Radio 2 audience.

Reputation – What Risk?

With whom does the BBC have a reputation, and which stakeholder relationships are most significant? Let's take these one by one. BBC management has a reputation with the Trustees which it needs to maintain, clearly any bad publicity it attracts will reflect badly on the trustees. The same goes for reputation with the regulator, Ofcom, who shares governance responsibility with the Trustees. Reputation with trustees and regulator is critical as demonstrable good governance is linked to sustaining the annual licence fee income. Government committees such as the Public Accounts Committee (PAC) also perform a regulatory role and have a bearing on the government's attitude to the BBC.

Listeners and viewers who are licence fee payers represent a very significant customer audience. In a free market with a wide choice, the BBC must offer attractive broadcast output to retain audiences. Traditional Radio 2 listeners will view certain output as more offensive than younger new listeners. Of those who had tuned in to the show in question – and knew what to expect – only a handful actually complained. The 40,000 complaints received over successive weeks came from those who had not actually heard the programme but were influenced by the media story whipped up by the Mail on Sunday.

Reputation is also important among producers and performers, who determine content and style, whether employees or contractors. Up to the scandal creativity was valued yet after the scandal, censorship became the watchword as the appetite for risk swung from high to low. Some highly talented staff left the BBC when they felt their role was no longer about nurturing new talent but policing output. Reputation in the broadcast industry among peers is important and as a result of this scandal the BBC will probably acquire a reputation as a risk averse broadcaster fearful of losing its licence fee income.

The Sachsgate scandal was not the first reputation damaging incident at the BBC, there had been others previously. A phone-in voting competition continued taking votes and caller revenue after the winner had been decided. A pet naming competition on a children's programme deliberately ignored the audience preference in favour of the production team choice. Broadcasting of offensive material should be a simple editorial matter, but in Sachsgate the BBC was slow to gauge public reaction and initially defended the broadcast decision. This scandal showed not just one error of judgement, but complacency and incompetence leading to questions of fitness for purpose from rival print media.

Risk Mitigation

What could be done to mitigate this type of risk in future? The most important stakeholder relationship for the BBC is its relationship with the government as it determines the continuity of public funding via the licence fee. For any organisation funded by the taxpayer demonstrating value for money is a key requirement and essential to mitigate reputation risk. BBC management needs to exhibit both prudence and sound judgement to an audience of politicians, regulators and audit committees extravagance is definitely out.

In terms of audiences and the public for whom the BBC has a remit to *'educate, inform and entertain'* the challenge is to deliver this in the context of increasingly well funded commercial competitors who can out-bid for broadcast rights for key events such as sports matches. The BBC needs to exploit the values of trust, reliability and accessibility inherent in its reputation among the British public as an 'auntie'.

At an operational level there is clearly a need for tighter control of contractors, many of whom are the private companies of celebrity presenters. Editorial control must lie with a management team that understands the values of the organisation and that broadcasting as a public service needs metrics beyond audience size and share of ratings.

Ultimately, protecting the reputation of the BBC requires a keen understanding of its core values and their relevance in the present and future marketplace for broadcast media. Success now is judged on international sales and format licensing of popular family shows like 'Strictly Come Dancing', rather than creative innovation. Entertain seems to be a more influential sibling than Educate and Inform, and there is evidently more risk in this area.

PRIVATE SECTOR

Reputation risk in the private sector manifests itself differently, especially for public companies where a loss of trust leads to a reduction in market value. This is reputation with one stakeholder group, investors. Although many analysts rely on rapid share price decline as a tangible indication of reputation damage, this is not the whole picture although understandably newsworthy. This is reputation management from the perspective of just one stakeholder group at one given moment in time. It excludes the reputation damage which will show as a future cost – declines in customer revenue, employee morale and supplier trust all have a cost that will impact in subsequent financial reports. Reputation risk is the risk to value not only in the short term but in the future, well after media interest has moved on.

The scale of risk is often only apparent too late. Gerald Ratner had no idea that his business empire would be damaged beyond repair by a quote taken out of context. Jarvis, the Railtrack contractor, had no idea that it would be so badly damaged after one small derailment. In each case the loss of customer confidence following a reputation damaging incident that business never fully recovered. Some organisations seem to ride crisis after crisis taking minor damage without causing a collapse in confidence. As we shall see these normally have little effective competition so customer displeasure cannot readily be expressed. Damage is relative but the risk is present and there are lessons in citing the case studies below.

2.1 BRITISH AIRWAYS

In March 2008 British Airways launched their service from a new passenger terminal at Heathrow, T5. Designed by Richard Rogers and opened by the Queen, the service was heralded as a state of the art passenger experience offering fast and efficient baggage handling. As everyone now knows the reality was that it couldn't deliver this on the first day with the result of flight delays and lost baggage. Embarrassing not only for the airline but for Britain as both incoming and outgoing passengers on scheduled routes were delayed. The logistical challenge of sorting out a backlog of baggage was so great that 30,000 passenger bags were eventually taken by road to Milan for sorting.

The system hadn't been adequately tested. On Day One critical baggage handling staff were prevented from reaching their work stations due to new security measures. Without the staff the new high technology baggage handling system, about which so much PR had focused, failed spectacularly within hours of opening for business. Passengers were separated from their bags and many flights took off without hold baggage. Incoming flights also suffered and the baggage kept piling up. The queues got longer and the world's media, on hand to cover the opening day, got their story but it wasn't the one BA had wanted.

British Airways, no longer the state airline, is a profitable airline offering a sound investment, better than many international rivals. It enjoys the positive association with British values through its brand name and heritage, but all this fell apart at the launch of T5. As one commentator at the time said: 'It has taken a good 20 years to get rid of a reputation of being a country paralysed by industrial action, who knows what long term image damage we are setting up when infrastructure projects like T5 appear so shambolic'. Over succeeding weeks the teething troubles were dealt with and some senior managers were fired, the share price fell a little and there were some calls for Willie Walsh to go but he weathered the storm.

Reputation – What Risk?

Investors were surprised by media coverage of the chaos but the share price didn't suffer too badly and most fund managers felt that BA had the right management at the helm, if not the right middle managers in place for the opening of T5. The city tended to see this as an operational blunder not indicative of deeper problems. Reputation among the investment community didn't suffer too badly. The sackings and internal enquiry halted the demand for blood, the shares were not significantly hit. It was not the same among staff and passengers.

Passengers were outraged by the fiasco and had every right to switch to rival airlines, some will never fly BA again. The BA reputation among the travelling public had been deteriorating slowly even before it ceased to claim to be the '*world's favourite airline*'. It has been said BA wins passengers because it controls so many good business routes and convenient time slots, not because it is any better than others in a commodity market. It has a reputation for losing baggage and it was partly to address this that so much was claimed about baggage handling at the T5 launch.

Staff and airport workers did not hold BA in high esteem prior to the T5 launch as Willie Walsh had been a cost cutter responsible for a large redundancy programme. The operational failures at T5 put the staff under enormous pressure in the front line facing customer anger, and many felt they were forced to cover up on the floor of the terminal for failures in management sitting comfortably beyond the reach of irate and frustrated passengers. Reputation among employees undoubtedly suffered from the T5 chaos as airline staff were asked to do an extremely difficult crisis management job under duress.

Risk Mitigation

In retrospect it was far too ambitious to expect a new terminal to work smoothly from day one. Lacking any phased switch from other terminals and lacking any real test runs the launch was a high risk in itself. It is said that some staff did point out the risk in advance but were ignored given the political momentum and hubris surrounding the royal opening. It is clear now that a full trial run ought to have been carried out which will be essential for any future terminal opening. Perhaps the desire to accommodate timetable pressure led to too many untested assumptions about capability. If so, this is common to many organisations when things go wrong.

It has also been said that the redundancy programme permitted too much knowledge and experience to exit the company at the worst possible time. Knowledge that is needed only once every 20 years for a major logistical operation departed on the eve of the terminal opening. Without knowing the detail of resources and capabilities it is hard to verify this, but it has been rumoured that this was a major contributor. If true then a key learning point is to conduct a skills audit in parallel with a redundancy programme to avoid knowledge gaps.

Apart from testing prior to launch and retaining key talent there is a third possible aspect of learning in all this. The plan to switch so much of BA Heathrow operations at one time was perhaps just not feasible. Here the learning is about realism and knowing what can be achieved. Not biting off more than can be chewed is one way of looking at it. Any change programme that consultants design is timed so that the pace of change suits the culture, too fast or too much and it doesn't work. Maybe the degree of change expected by BA was unrealistic but nobody wanted to be the person to delay the royal opening?

2.2 SEVERN TRENT WATER

When the government decided to privatise the water industry in the UK it set up Water and Sewage Companies (WASCOs) of which Severn Trent was one. Each private company could set charges for water supply and sewage disposal to both domestic and commercial customers subject to meeting certain performance criteria set by the water regulator Ofwat. Price increases could only be justified if supported by evidence from among other metrics, high levels of customer satisfaction and low levels of leakage from the mains network. Severn Trent water produced evidence of these to justify price increases but was found to have falsified the evidence, resulting in a fine from Ofwat and prosecution by the Serious Fraud Office (SFO).

In July 2008 Ofwat fined Severn Trent £35.8 million for deliberately providing false information and for delivering poor service to its customers. Although a record fine it represented under 3 per cent of the water company's turnover. The Ofwat statement expressed it strongly:

Severn Trent Water's behaviour was unacceptable. The size of the fine reflects how seriously Ofwat takes the deliberate misreporting of information. This sends a clear message to the company and to the rest of the water sector – Ofwat will protect consumers and companies must comply with their legal obligations or pay the price. Any further attempts to deliberately mislead Ofwat could lead to even bigger fines ...

The SFO prosecution of Severn Trent Water related to two offences of supplying false data about leakage to Ofwat and is not connected to the Ofwat investigation into misreporting customer service information. Together the prosecution for fraud and the Ofwat fine combined to seriously damage the water company's reputation.

Reputation – What Risk?

Investors react cautiously to regulator intervention as it indicates a concern over management competence and good governance. They react with even more concern when the Serious Fraud Office takes an interest as this indicates misfeasance or malfeasance, either way the criminal act of fraud is an unequivocal investment deterrent. Reputation with investors is at risk when regulator and SFO are involved. Shareholders will not be pleased with the Ofwat decision:

Severn Trent Water's shareholders will bear the entire cost of the proposed penalty. It cannot be passed on to its customers.

Reputation as an ethical investment similarly suffered. In the 2008 Co-Operative Asset Management (CAM) ethical company ranking Severn Trent fell from 15 in the FTSE 350 to 159 entirely due to its reputation for fraudulent practices.

Reputation with customers is also at stake although many are unable to switch supplier as with electricity and gas provision. Reputation with customers will not have been helped by revelations such as:

> *Severn Trent Water's Customer Relations Department deliberately misreported some of its customer service data to hide its true performance in 2005 and in earlier years.*

Reputation among rival water companies will have suffered to some degree as the fine was a record for the industry reflecting the dissatisfaction of the regulator.

Risk Mitigation

In April 2008 once the regulator had determined the fine Severn Trent put out the following contrite press release (http://www.stwater.co.uk/server.php?show=ConWebDoc .3403). The company accepted full responsibility and acted quickly to restore investor confidence.

The following day a further press release set out to distance the current management regime from a past one at fault (http:// www.stwater.co.uk/server.php?show=ConWebDoc.3404). The aim was to show that from March 2005 the new regime had been keen to put things right.

With regard to the SFO *The Times* in November 2007 reported:

Severn Trent will be the first utility to be prosecuted by the SFO when it charges the company with three offences, relating to alleged misreporting of data on leaks to the water regulator between 2000 and 2002.

This news is also covered under a press release from Severn Trent reflecting the policy of transparency among the new management team (http://www.stwater.co.uk/server.php?show=ConWebDoc.3269). A websearch of the outcome only reveals an undated press release (presumably post April 2008) from Severn Trent about an SFO fine of £2m (http://www.severntrent.com/server.php?show=ConWebDoc.434).

Mitigating the reputation risk involves contrition and clear distance from the old regime. The fines themselves are less important than the message sent to the rest of the industry and investors. Customers, sadly, don't get a lot of choice so the reputation risk sits mainly with investors.

There are two issues here, regulator compliance and fraud investigation. Damage from regulator fines depend on the nature of the transgression and in this case the regulator was particularly concerned about the deliberate deception. Accidental breach of a regulator code is probably less damaging to reputation than a deliberate breach.

Interest from the SFO is another matter and moves into the realm of business ethics as fraud is essentially a criminal matter. Any organisation dependent on the trust of investors, employees, customers and other key stakeholders must avoid laying itself open to questions of its integrity and honesty. The suggestion of fraud can be almost as damaging as a conviction.

2.3 BAE SYSTEMS

British Aerospace is a major manufacturer of weapons for the arms industry and a highly successful British corporation in the global Defence systems marketplace. The industry is secretive, its lack of transparency means it is shunned by ethical investors as it is hard to make a case for 'doing good' from weapon sales. Responsible manufacturers do not sell weapons to political regimes likely to use weapons for the repression of internal unrest rather than defence from external aggression. However there is no doubt that the sales process is murky, especially in regimes where officials with power to influence decisions are reputed only to progress a tender if it includes their own 'arrangement fee' paid directly into a private offshore bank account.

Anyone who has tried to sell goods in markets outside Europe knows that the business ethics of British or American investors simply do not operate. Since 1985 when a major BAE contract with Saudi Arabia, known as 'Al Yamamah' was won by the Thatcher government, the SFO had been investigating the possibility that this was secured through bribery of key Saudi officials. In 2007 UK investigators from the SFO finally secured permission from the Swiss authorities to examine the bank records of Saudi officials thought to be involved in the Al Yamamah deal. Within days the Prime Minister Tony Blair halted the SFO investigation.

The UK government claimed that Saudi Arabia, displeased with such intrusion into private bank records, would suspend co-operation on intelligence sharing with the UK thus rendering the UK less safe from terrorism. This might have been convincing if within weeks a new and very lucrative BAE contract with Saudi Arabia known as 'Salam' had not been won. It was clear to even the most gullible journalist that the SFO had been called off to protect the new deal which was near to completion. In order to regain some credibility BAE conducted its own ethical audit under the highly respected Lord Woolf. The Woolf report came out in May 2008 and was not the whitewash that had been expected, containing as it did some criticism of BAE's secrecy.

Reputation – What Risk?

There is no specific reputation threatening incident at stake here. Investors and customers have not yet been deterred by a long running investigation in the UK by the Fraud Office and a handful of investigative journalists. Customers tend to be national governments seeking to equip their own armed forces, weapons performance is a key purchase decision. Most people who operate in this market accept that deals have to be sensitively set up and that a forensic accountancy trail is usually unwelcome.

The Woolf report did however give concern in the UK and US where government tends to play three distinct stakeholder interest roles: First is law maker giving licence to operate or export, second is regulator setting standards for commercial interests and industry behaviour, and third is customer through the Ministry of Defence (UK) and Department of Defense (US). Government relations are very important to an arms manufacturer and there is a very strong awareness of the need to protect reputation with this multi-faceted stakeholder.

Any hint of unethical dealing will impact on reputation with the government department approving a licence to operate and manufacture goods for export. This is the most important stakeholder to the arms manufacturer and one with whom good relations are essential. Under no circumstances must this relationship be jeopardised. Beyond this customers are of course important where winning contracts in the face of foreign competition is often as much about politics as price or performance.

The risk to reputation with the UK government exists while the SFO continues to investigate possible bribery claims regarding past arms deals. Once a retired company officer claims to have proof that a deal was secured through a secret private payment, then the government must not be seen to condone this type of business conduct. At this point there will need to be a line drawn between principle and practice.

Risk Mitigation

When faced with accusations of unethical behaviour or bribery there are only really two alternatives. One is to deny it and demonstrate transparent business practice, invite any regulator to investigate fully and deliver a verdict to clear your name with all significant stakeholders. The other alternative is to admit that it had occurred in the past but changes in personnel and policies mean that the organisation is now 'clean'.

The Woolf committee could have achieved the former for BAE but their remit was restricted to exclude past behaviour, thus compounding the suspicion among critics that there had been some unethical practices in the past. An opportunity to follow the alternative strategy and signal a break with the past presented itself in the summer of 2007 when the MD retired, but this was not exploited in relations with either the SFO (UK) or Department of Justice (US).

Unfortunately like a dog with a bone, the SFO is still pursuing BAE through other markets – for example, in December 2008 the SFO gained access to Swiss bank account details relating to a an aborted BAE deal with the Czech Republic in 2001. Meanwhile in the US the Department of Justice still has unfinished business with BAE. Damage is ongoing while both SFO and DoJ are pursuing the company, so the risk to reputation exists until these regulatory bodies have achieved closure on their enquiries. Mitigation can only be successful if regulator satisfaction is a top priority, the longer enquiries go on the greater the potential damage.

Bibliography

REPUTATION RISK

BOOKS

1. *Corporate Reputation* – Garry Honey and Arlo Brady (2007) published by CIMA.

2. *Reputational Risk, A Question of Trust* – Lynn Drennan, Derek Atkins and Ian Bates (2006) published by Lessons Publishing.

3. *Ethicability* – Roger Steare (2006) published by Roger Steare Consulting.

4. *Fame and Fortune: How Successful Companies Build Winning Reputations* – Fombrun and Van Riel (2006) published by Prentice Hall.

5. *The Sustainability Effect, Rethinking Corporate Reputation in the 21st Century* – Arlo Brady (2005) published by Palgrave.

6. *Trust Matters* – Bibb and Kourdi (2004) published by Palgrave.

7. *The Timid Corporation* – Benjamin Hunt (2003) published by Wiley.

8. *Strategic Reputation Risk Management* – Judy Larkin (2003) published by Palgrave.

9. *CEO Capital: A Guide to Building CEO Reputation and Company Success* – Leslie Gaines-Ross (2002) published by Wiley.

10. *Risk, Crisis and Security Management* – Ed Borodzicz (2005) published by Wiley.

11. *Managing Reputational Risk* – Jenny Rayner (2003) published by Wiley.

12. *Corporate Reputation and Competitiveness* – Gary Davies (2003) published by Routledge.

13. *Invisible Advantage – How Intangibles are Driving Business Performance* – Jonathan Low and Pam Cohen Kalafut (2002) published by Perseus Publishing.

14. *Waltzing with Raptors* – Glen Peters (1999) published by Wiley.

15. *Reputation: Realizing Value from the Corporate Image* – Fombrun (1996) published by Harvard Business School Press.

PAPERS

1. *The Risk Management of Everything, Rethinking the Politics of Uncertainty* – Michael Power (2004) published by Demos.

2. *The Orange Book – Management of Risk Principles and Concepts* (2004) published by HM Treasury.

3. *Risk Management at the Crossroads* – Richard Sharman (March 2003) published in *Management Quarterly*.

4. *The Evolving Role of the CRO* (2005) published by the Economic Intelligence Unit.

5. *Best Practice in Risk Management* (2007) published by the Economic Intelligence Unit.

6. *Reputation: Risk of Risks* (2005) published by the Economic Intelligence Unit.

7. *BS 31100 Code of Practice for Risk Management* (2008) published by the British Standards Institute.

OTHER READING

1. *Black Swan* – Nassim Taleb (2007) published by Allen Lane.

2. *Risk, The Science and Politics of Fear* – Dan Gardner (2008) published by Virgin Books.

3. *The Ascent of Money: A Financial History of the World* – Niall Ferguson (2008) published by Tantor Media.

4. *Brand Risk* – David Abrahams (2008) published by Gower Publishing.

If you have found this book useful you may be interested in other titles from Gower

Supply Chain Risk
Edited by
Clare Brindley
Hardback: 978-0-7546-3902-2

The Complete Guide to Business Risk Management
Kit Sadgrove
Hardback: 978-0-566-08661-8

Risk-Based Auditing
Phil Griffiths
Hardback: 978-0-566-08652-6
e-book: 978-0-7546-8309-4

Information Risk and Security:
Preventing and Investigating Workplace Computer Crime
Edward Wilding
Hardback: 978-0-566-08685-4

Understanding and Managing Risk Attitude
David Hillson and Ruth Murray-Webster
Paperback: 978-0-566-08798-1

Estimating Risk:
A Management Approach
Andy Garlick
Hardback: 978-0-566-08776-9

GOWER

Brand Risk:
Adding Risk Literacy to Brand Management
David Abrahams
Hardback: 978-0-566-08724-0
e-book: 978-0-7546-8890-7

Intelligent Internal Control and Risk Management:
Designing High-Performance Risk Control Systems
Matthew Leitch
Hardback: 978-0-566-08799-8
e-book: 978-0-7546-8893-8

Managing Group Risk Attitude:
Ruth Murray-Webster and David Hillson
Hardback: 978-0-566-08787-5
e-book: 978-0-7546-8135-9

Practical Schedule Risk Analysis
David Hulett
Hardback: 978-0-566-08790-5
e-book: 978-0-7546-9196-9

Managing Risk in Projects
David Hillson
Paperback: 978-0-566-08867-4
e-book: 978-0-566-09155-1

Visit **www.gowerpublishing.com/risk** and

- search the entire catalogue of Gower books in print
- order titles online at 10% discount
- take advantage of special offers
- sign up for our monthly e-mail update service
- download free sample chapters from all recent titles
- download or order our catalogue